Launch the Lifeboat to Read and Spell

Book 1

Lifeboat
Book 1

First edition published by The Robinswood Press 2000

© Jacqueline Davison, Michael Davison,
Sula Ellis and Tony Ellis 2000

Sula Ellis, Tony Ellis, Jacqueline Davison and Michael Davison
have asserted their rights under the Copyright, Designs and
Patents Act 1988 to be identified as the authors of this work.

Design and illustrations:
© Stephen Emms, Phil Goundrey, George Marshall and
The Robinswood Press 2000.

This version (v1.4) printed by Blueprint Design & Graphics Limited.

All rights reserved. No part of this publication may be reproduced,
stored in a retrieval system or transmitted in any form, or by any means,
electronic, mechanical, photocopying, recording or otherwise,
without the prior permission in writing from the publisher.

The publisher, however, hereby authorises individual specialist, literacy and
other teachers to take, without the prior permission in writing of the publisher,
photocopies of any pages from this book for use exclusively in teaching and
homework situations within the limits of one teaching establishment only.

The Robinswood Press

Malvern   England
www.robinswoodpress.com

ISBN 1-869981-626

Contents

Page

FOREWORD	5
TEACHING GUIDE	6
Introduction	6
The Lesson Format	10
Lifeboat Programme Structure	14
Assessment Sheets	16
Lifeboat Record Chart	18
Student Progress Chart	19
Certificate of Achievement	19
LESSON NOTES TO BOOK 1	20

BOOK 1 WORKSHEETS

Lesson

1	**Alphabet Sequencing**	22
2	**Consonants**	30
3	**Vowels**	38
4	**i**	46
5	**i n p s t**	54
6	**a**	62
7	**b d**	70
8	**sn sp st**	78
9	**-nd -nt**	86
10	**Review and Post-test**	94

ANSWERS TO BOOK 1 LESSONS

Lesson

1	**Alphabet Sequencing**	102
2	**Consonants**	104
3	**Vowels**	106
4	**i**	108
5	**i n p s t**	110
6	**a**	112
7	**b d**	114
8	**sn sp st**	116
9	**-nd -nt**	118
10	**Review and Post-test**	120

About the Authors

Sula Ellis BA (Hons) PGCE (Distinction) DipSpLD (Dyslexia Institute) AMBDA
Tony Ellis MBA BEng DipSpLD (Hornsby International Dyslexia Centre)

Sula and Tony Ellis of *Ellis Dyslexia Consultants* have many years' combined experience as Special Needs teachers, running units in Berkshire and Surrey in addition to tutoring in both the state and private sectors. Sula Ellis has taught as an OCR lecturer at East Berkshire College, training teachers to Diploma level in Special Needs. She is completing doctoral research in Dyslexia and Mathematics with Professor TR Miles, University of Wales, Bangor and Professor TJ Wheeler, Principal of University College, Chester.

Jackie Davison BTech (Hons) DipSpLD (Hornsby International Dyslexia Centre)
Mick Davison DipSpLD (Hornsby International Dyslexia Centre)

Jackie and Mick Davison are based in Hertfordshire where they provide a successful Learning Support service through *Davison Dyslexia Tutors.* They are directly involved in specialist teaching for a large number of pupils, generally in the age range of 7 to 13 years.

Acknowledgements

The production of a work of this magnitude required considerable support from colleagues and other professionals in the area of Special Needs who provided encouragement, advice, expertise and appraisal.

The authors would particularly like to thank teachers from the two hundred Berkshire schools who took part in the original MBA research project, which led to the development of the Lifeboat scheme, by completing questionnaires and providing practical guidance on their needs; Jan Donlon for the extensive typing task; Matthew Turner, for suggesting the title; and all the many students who, during the trial period of *Lifeboat,* have given us such constructive feedback.

The title – *Launch the Lifeboat to Read and Spell* – derives from the ex-RNLI Watson Class lifeboat which, after helping to save 160 lives while in service at Southend-on-Sea and Beaumaris, became the authors' headquarters for the development and realisation of this scheme. It deserved its own special acknowledgement.

Foreword

It gives me great pleasure to commend this Resource Pack. I know it to be based on the authors' many years' experience in the teaching of dyslexic children and on their knowledge of what these children are likely to find difficult. Moreover, this Pack so obviously represents 'good practice' that one can recommend it as being suitable for teaching reading and spelling to *all* children, whether dyslexic or not. I have never seen dyslexic children as a 'race apart': as I see the situation, it is simply that non-dyslexic children pick many things up for themselves which dyslexic children need to have carefully explained to them.

This is how the authors themselves describe the programme: *"the lesson topics are highly structured to present spelling rules, specific letter blends and phonics in a multi-sensory way"*. There is, in fact, wide agreement among teachers in the English-speaking world that a programme of this kind is the most appropriate and effective one for dyslexic individuals of all ages who are struggling to become literate. The present Resource Pack is innovative, however, in that it allows class teachers to teach the class as a whole in advance of the time when the children will be working at their own workbooks. This seems to me highly cost effective use of teachers' time: it combines the social advantages of group work with the opportunity for children to have their own individualised programmes and progress at their own speed.

To all who use the Resource Pack, teachers and students alike, I send my good wishes.

Professor TR Miles MA PhD CPsychol FBPsS

Now that all children are expected to be included in the mainstream classroom, it is most appropriate that this resource pack has been made available, based on the principles espoused by the founders of the 'multi-sensory' approach to teaching SpLD and dyslexic students. With this scheme, the 20 per cent who have always found difficulty with reading, writing, spelling – and sometimes mathematics - will have an opportunity to learn more easily. It is only by targeting the 20 per cent that true literacy across the range of those at risk can ever be achieved. Of course, those with severe problems will probably still need extra help, but at least this will be in line with that being taught in the classroom rather than in conflict with traditional teaching.

In addition, this scheme is applicable to all age groups from primary through secondary into tertiary and adult dyslexic units. It therefore not only makes integration possible – it also benefits those without any learning difficulties by teaching them grammar, punctuation and sentence construction.

Professor Bevé Hornsby
MBE PhD MSc MEd FRCSLT AFBPsS HonFCP FRSA AMBDA

Teaching Guide – Introduction

Background

It is generally acknowledged that there are many more students these days who need help with their literacy skills. Whether the increase is the result of environmental or social factors or the fact that the diagnosis of special needs has become far more effective and 'acceptable', the consequence – in the classroom – of this growth is yet more pressure for literacy teachers.

There is a fine tradition of research and remediation for certain special needs difficulties. The need for a *multi-sensory* approach was recognised initially through the Orton Gillingham developments in the USA. In the UK, a more *structured* and *systematic* approach to language teaching was encouraged by Kathleen Hickey, Bevé Hornsby, Helen Arkell and Tim Miles. These principles were adopted by the Dyslexia Institute, the BDA, the Bangor Dyslexia Unit and the Hornsby and Arkell Centres, all of which provide excellent training in diagnosis or in the specialist teaching methods required by those responsible for special needs.

The specialist programmes available to schools, however, usually require both a specialist teacher, and either one-to-one attention or work with small groups out of the classroom. Whilst this highly effective and dedicated work is essential for some situations, the approach can be both costly, and disruptive for general class work for the pupil. It also largely precludes potential input from other support staff and parents. Moreover, the programmes generally do little to assist the classroom teacher in the need for *differentiated* work, given the range of capabilities that is the reality in most classrooms, especially during The Literacy Hour.

The need was evident, therefore, for a resource which would be suitable for general use in the classroom in addition to these specialist situations. Such a scheme would need to be *comprehensive, structured, cumulative* and *multi-sensory*, suitable for *differentiated* work in the classroom, acceptable to the wide age range of potential students, and *user-friendly* – that is, capable of being managed not just by the specialist, but also by the class teacher, the classroom assistant and parents.

The programme 'Launch the Lifeboat to Read and Spell' was developed to meet this specification by Ellis Dyslexia Consultants, following research and consultation with a large number of teaching staff in schools throughout Berkshire, England. Trials in schools showed the approach to be highly successful in both content and presentation. Students using the scheme have made significant gains in literacy skills and have consequently grown in confidence. The Lifeboat scheme has therefore been received enthusiastically by teachers, parents and students alike.

The Lifeboat Scheme – Structured, Comprehensive and Cumulative

The scheme was designed to help develop the reading and spelling skills of *all* students. Great care was taken in its development to ensure the requirements of the general classroom were met, especially for independent and differentiated work, and the need for a precise, step-by-step, accumulative approach for students identified as requiring specialist tuition in order to grasp the essentials of the English language.

The Lifeboat scheme meets these requirements by being entirely self-contained and by having a highly structured, comprehensive programme, presented in a standard format of multi-sensory exercises. The Lesson Format is introduced in detail on pages 10 to 13, and the programme itself is laid out in the Lifeboat Programme Structure on pages 14 to 15. The Programme Structure is an important reference source for users, and has been designed so that it can be used as a wall chart for easy access.

Lifeboat lessons progress in a sequential, step-by-step manner which brings a deeper understanding of phonics used in the English language. Each lesson covers just one topic, and incorporates only those phonics, letters and blends which have been covered in previous lessons. This gives the student the opportunity to build cumulatively on earlier groundwork and establishes the potential for continual 'success' for the student. Topics on vowels, digraphs, blends, diphthongs, prefixes, suffixes and syllables are thus presented in a structure that carefully builds from the very early stages to more demanding concepts.

Multi-sensory Approach

The format of the Lifeboat worksheets and the approach used in individual exercises draws on the principles of *multi-sensory* teaching methods recommended, for example, by the British Dyslexia Association. It is felt that the most successful way to help students with literacy difficulties at any level is with exercises requiring *visual, kinaesthetic* and *auditory* sensory channels. 'Speaking' aloud, becoming 'involved' with a particular sound, as well as simply 'looking' at letters and words on the page all help the student to gain command and knowledge.

The result of this approach is that students are much more likely to learn effective strategies with which to overcome their areas of difficulty and which assist them to recall information from memory more efficiently. As a consequence, the individual student may come to access the richness of the English language with far greater depth and with a more satisfying sense of achievement.

'User-friendly' Format

The structure of the programme and the format of the individual lessons have been designed with the need for independent working in mind. The format of the worksheets remains consistent, after a few introductory lessons in Book 1, and this contributes to the ease with which students can work on their own. Although it is always valuable to have recourse to trained specialist staff, the scheme is straightforward to operate and the student's progress can be quite easily monitored with the materials supplied. It can therefore be managed very successfully not only by the specialist, but also by the classroom teacher, the classroom assistant and by parents themselves.

The user is referred to as 'student' throughout, since those who will benefit from the scheme are in a wide age range: from primary school children to secondary, further and higher education students, adult learners, those with English as a second language, etc. The exercises have been designed to appeal across this range.

Differentiated Work and The Literacy Hour

Since the Lifeboat programme can be used by all school children, and since the actual layout enables each student to work independently, the scheme can be used *differentially* by the whole class in a group setting. It is therefore invaluable for work during The Literacy Hour, especially since Lifeboat includes exercises which improve skills at word, sentence and text levels. Once pupils have become familiar with the worksheet format they may also work on the lessons unsupervised, whether at school or at home. The lessons can therefore be used for independent study, holiday work and reading homework.

Essential Elements of the Lifeboat Scheme

Overview

The Lifeboat scheme consists of 10 spiral-bound, photocopiable books, each of which contains 10 lessons. Each lesson consists of eight worksheets, with each worksheet occupying a full A4 page. From Lesson 8 in Book 1, the layout of each lesson is identical, providing continuity and confidence – and the consequent option of independent, unsupervised work.

Design and Layout

The front covers have been designed to help remind users of the sequential nature of the set. A small lifeboat makes its way across the covers from Book 1 to Book 10. A rainbow colour sequence also runs across Books 1 to 8. Books 9 and 10 are tinted to reflect their influence on Books 4 to 7. The number of each book is displayed down the leading edge of the cover to assist in quick location of a desired title from a shelf full of indistinguishable wire spirals!

The Lifeboat worksheets are illustrated in a way which will appeal to a wide audience. The text and the illustrations often represent some quite sophisticated ideas and display humour and a sense of fun. The text is printed in a larger point size in Books 1 to 5, and the printed Assessment sheets adopt a similar format. Each page is numbered at the bottom with the book page number and with the relevant number for the Book, the Lesson, and the Lesson Page. This feature is of great assistance in keeping photocopies in place.

Teaching Guide

This is contained in Book 1. Since most users have access to the full scheme, it was felt unnecessary to print these pages in each book. Much of the Guide is available on the Internet, on: www.robinswood.co.uk and can be printed out. The Guide contains the Lesson Format, the Lifeboat Programme Structure, two Assessment sheets, the Lifeboat Record Chart, a Student Progress Chart and a Certificate of Achievement. All items in the Lifeboat scheme are photocopiable for use within one institution by administrators of the Lifeboat scheme, and by students for both class and home work.

Book 1

Book One is for the beginner. It introduces the alphabet and distinguishes the vowels and the consonants, in a series of individually designed lessons. This stage obviously requires teaching support. Later lessons focus upon the letters i, n, p, s, t, a, b, d and h, which give rise to blends 'sn', 'sp', 'st', '-nd' and '-nt'. Lessons 6, 8, 9 and 10 introduce the learner to the lesson design consistent to the remaining books.

Books 2 to 8

Each lesson in Books 2 to 8 covers a different topic. Worksheets highlight spelling rules and specific letter blends and sounds. These seven books, containing 70 lessons, provide the essential coverage of the elements of the English language. A detailed description of each of the eight worksheets is given in the Lesson Format on pages 10 to 13.

Books 9 and 10

These books present some key spelling rules and other intricate spelling patterns which are particularly essential for whole class work and which complement the topics in Books 4 to 7. These lesson topics, such as 'Doubling Letters', 'Prefixes', 'Soft 'g' (j) Sound' and 'Silent Letters' have been selected for special treatment because of their complexity and due to their general importance to the English language. To maintain the integrity of the cumulative, structured approach, the lessons in these two books should be presented sequentially to dovetail with lessons throughout Books 4 to 7, as shown in the Lifeboat Programme Structure on pages 14 to 15. The Review at the end of Book 10 encompasses the Whole Scheme.

Review and Post-test Lessons

In line with the Whole Scheme Review of Book 10, the last lesson – Lesson 10 – in Books 1 to 8 is a Review and Post-test, which consolidates all previous work in the scheme. These can also be used for assessment.

'Challenge' Words

'Challenge' words are included in the lessons. These are words which do not follow the usual rules *(odd words)* or the usual sounds *(sight words)* – often called 'helping' words. 'Challenge' words also refer to words which include elements only covered in a *later* topic *(early words)*. Generally, *odd words* are indicated with an asterisk (*) on the first page of the lesson in which they appear (above the tracking exercise). Common *sight words,* such as: 'was', 'their', 'are', 'who', 'your', 'said', 'very', 'where', 'were', 'many' and 'here', and *early words,* which appear out of structure, are listed in the Lesson Notes, with the challenging part of the word underlined. Some place and country names in the text fall into these categories.

Lesson Notes

A more detailed introduction to each lesson topic, including spelling rules, sounds and challenge words – *sight words* and *'early words'* – is found in each book just before Lesson 1.

Answers

To assist the marking of work (whether by the teacher, assistant, parent or student), answers for each page are included at the end of every book. These have been completed in cursive handwriting.

Using the Lifeboat Scheme

The Lesson Format   Lifeboat Programme Structure   Lesson Notes

The Lesson Format on pages 10 to 13 provides teachers with details of the *Skill Aims* of each worksheet, a *Summary* of the exercise(s) concerned, and some *Golden Teaching Tips*, which may assist in enriching lesson presentation. The Lifeboat Programme Structure, on pages 14 and 15, is an overview of the entire Lifeboat scheme showing contents of each book and how the Lessons in Books 9 and 10 are inserted. The Lesson Notes, contained in each book individually, provide more details of the content of each lesson.

Assessment

Many users of the Lifeboat scheme will follow the full programme from Book 1 onwards without recourse to initial assessment. Where students have already started a literacy programme but are to change to the Lifeboat scheme, it is important to establish their existing skill base in *spelling* and *reading*. A change may occur on a whole class basis, perhaps because of the differentiated work possibilities with these worksheets. An individual student may change when identified as having some difficulty with literacy. In either case, the Assessment sheets on pages 16 and 17, which link directly with the programme structure, will be helpful.

The assessment of *spelling* is generally far more important and revealing. It can be administered in either whole class, group or individual settings and, to achieve a good overview of the student's capabilities, it is recommended that the administrator adopts the following guidelines:

- i)   Keep the Assessment sheets out of the student's sight!
- ii) Say the spelling word.
- iii) Incorporate the word into a meaningful sentence.
- iv) Repeat the spelling word clearly.
- vi) Allow the student enough time to write down the word.

Both Assessment sheets are laid out similarly but provide the opportunity for varied assessment to prevent familiarity and over-learning. The Assessments sheets comprise groups of 10 words sequentially chosen from each lesson of each Lifeboat book, totalling 100 words. The book reference is printed down the left side of the sheet. This tool will highlight the areas of difficulty experienced by the student and the positive skill level. Thus the most appropriate starting point in the Lifeboat scheme for each individual or group can be identified. This knowledge also enables the class teacher to group students with similar skills, and to draw up Education Plans as necessary.

When used as a *reading* assessment, the Assessment sheet needs to be presented on an individual basis. The student should read out loud along the lines from the left to right starting at the top. (Note that the point size for the Assessment sheets printed from the web site does not reduce for Books 6 to 10.)

The sheets can be re-used later, either as a spelling or reading assessment, to review the progress and knowledge consolidation of the student.

Marking

It is preferable to use positive marking rather than 'crosses' denoting incorrect responses. Students usually do put a lot of effort into their work and deserve to be praised and encouraged for their achievements.

Recording and Rewarding Progress

The Lifeboat Record Chart provides the teacher, parent or student with a recording sheet covering the entire Lifeboat Programme Structure. It should be used to highlight specific areas of weakness discovered in the assessment and can be used as a running record of progress through the scheme.

The Progress Chart is provided for the student to keep their own record of books or lessons completed. Colours or stickers can be used to enhance the appeal of this. Each dark spot on the Chart represents one lesson. Once a lesson has been completed, the next dark spot can be coloured or a sticker placed on it.

Finally, a Certificate is provided as an award for the completion of each group of lessons or book.

Teaching Guide – The Lesson Format

From Lesson 8, Book 1, the format of every lesson remains consistent. This gives the student continuity and it fosters independent learning, which can take place during The Literacy Hour. Every lesson consists of eight worksheets, each occupying a full page, which are carefully laid out to achieve particular objectives around the specific lesson topic. The goal is to challenge the student – in a multi-sensory, fun and exciting way – with concepts and ideas, grammar and punctuation, phonic awareness and comprehension. The start of each lesson is indicated by a lifeboat alongside the topic title. To help with organisation, the book, lesson and page number are printed at the bottom of every page.

The techniques and principles used in the Lifeboat scheme help students to gain knowledge of language skills which will be effectively stored in their memory for speedy and accurate retrieval. Learning through this scheme develops a clearer understanding of our complex but delightfully versatile language. The illustrations on pages 10 to 13 are taken from Books 2, 3, 4, 7 and 10.

Page 1 Introduction and Tracking

Skill Aims Reading for Meaning Visual Perceptual Skills
Hand-eye Coordination Fine Motor Control

Summary

The first worksheet introduces the topic relevant to the whole lesson. Where appropriate, the heading area also carries useful hints on the topic. A space has been left for the student to add their name.

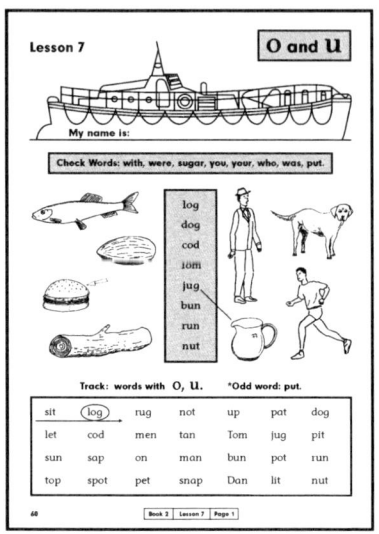

The box in the centre of page 1 contains several specifically chosen words, in structure, connected to the lesson topic. The student joins the words to the pictures to demonstrate that they have *read for meaning*.

The page also carries a tracking task. This *visual perceptual* exercise helps the student to improve *hand-eye coordination* and *fine motor control* whilst learning to track around the specific words or letters.

The page may include *odd words* or 'rule-breakers'. These may make an odd or unusual sound, or they may break the more usual grammatical rules. These additions are marked with an asterisk (*).

Golden Teaching Tips

- Tracking task – check that the student circles the appropriate words or letters with an anti-clockwise sweep to maintain fluency and control.
- Discuss the *sound* involved and the rule where appropriate.
- Use different colours for tracking, for example, where two sounds or groups of letters are involved.
- Encourage accuracy from the student when tracking a word or if colouring in the illustrations – for *fine motor control* practice.

Page 2 Word Match

Skill Aim Visual Recognition

Summary

On this page, the student's task is to match eight trigger words to their partners which are hidden amongst other carefully chosen, but potentially confusing, words. All the words included on the page are in structure and many have been selected with the dyslexic person in mind, for example, words such as: 'step', 'set', 'tip' and 'stand'.

The trigger word is in the left hand column. The student should use *visual recognition* to compare the words in each row with the trigger word and circle the identical one.

Golden Teaching Tips

- The pupil or student could be encouraged to read aloud all the words before beginning the task.

Page 3 Spell and Write

Skill Aims   *Phonological Awareness   Cursive Handwriting*
                   Visual and Auditory Skills

Summary

This exercise trains *phonological awareness* through phoneme, morpheme and syllable separation. Particular words have been chosen in structure and according to the student's stage of syllable knowledge. These have been broken into their two or three phoneme, morpheme or syllable constituents which have then been hidden amongst other similar word components.

By combining both *visual and auditory skills,* the student is able to select from the correct set of word parts and so compile the whole word suggested by the illustration. Word parts are set in two or three rows to encourage both horizontal and vertical visual activity.

The student circles an appropriate word part from each row then writes the complete word in neat *cursive handwriting* in the space provided.

Golden Teaching Tips

- Encourage the student to sound out each component part of the discovered word whilst writing it in cursive form.
- Ensure that the student writes on the line provided, leading in and leading out of the word.
- Guide the student to sharpen their observation skills for capital letters, which serve as clues, where appropriate.

Page 4 Read and Choose

Skill Aim   *Reading and Comprehension Skills*

Summary

This task is in the form of a multiple choice exercise in which the student studies two sentences and chooses the one that best fits the illustration positioned between them. The worksheet is designed to strengthen the *reading and comprehension skills* of the student.

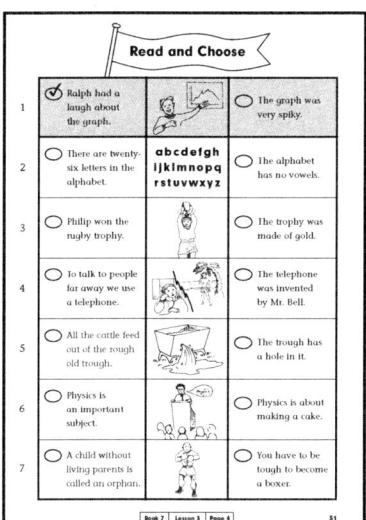

Both sentences are in structure and of similar construction, with closely matched word content. The student must, therefore, read both lines carefully before making a decision on the appropriate sentence. The choice is indicated by marking the circle alongside the correct sentence.

Golden Teaching Tips

- Guide the student to read both sentences first.
- Punctuation could be highlighted.
- Encourage the student to identify parts of speech such as nouns and verbs.

Page 5 Dictation or Look – Say – Cover – Write – Check

Skill Aims   Dictation   Cursive Handwriting
                Memory Training   Proof-reading
                Kinaesthetic Memory

Summary

This page carries a number of sentences, written in structure, which develop a sense of grammar and punctuation. The activity can be given in different ways and it is suitable for independent, group or class work.

The student needs to remember each sentence either after hearing it through *dictation* by the teacher or parent, or by reading it and saying it aloud. The student covers the sentence and then writes it down. This helps with both *memory training* and practice in *cursive handwriting*. The student can then *proof-read* their written work by uncovering the original sentence and checking their version against it.

The second part of this worksheet requires accurate copying, on the lines provided, of carefully selected letters or words. These may reflect other areas of the school curriculum, such as scientific, geographic and exam-orientated type words. Whilst writing, the student should take care to begin each letter group on the line, as advocated in specialist training.

The handwriting should conform to the following framework:

i) The writing should be in a consistent style, for example: Lower case *a b c*

   Upper case A B C

The style illustrated, which is recommended for learning support use, has been adopted throughout the Lifeboat scheme, and is encountered initially in Book 1, Lesson 2.

(Sufficient space has been left on the worksheets for the tutor or teacher to write their own style of cursive handwriting if found more appropriate.)

ii) Capital letters should not be joined to following letters. For example: *Stan*.

Golden Teaching Tips

- A further exercise can be conducted in the Handwriting section if required. Place the writing implement on a line of the worksheet. The student then closes their eyes and writes the letter/s or words using their tactile, or *kinaesthetic* skills. Remember to dot i's and cross any t's before opening the eyes.

- Encourage the student to practise cursive letters by writing on a variety of textured surfaces, such as a table top, their own hand, or even in the air ('sky-writing').

- Ask the student to draw pictures derived from the sentences to confirm their understanding.

Page 6 Listening Skills

Skill Aims   *Listening Skills*   *Auditory Discrimination*

Summary

Three words are presented one at a time, either visually or read out by the tutor or teacher. The student needs to identify an odd word out based on *sound* or *auditory discrimination* and state how they perceive the other two as being alike. All words are in structure and include a high percentage of lesson topic words. In addition, other words have been included for review.

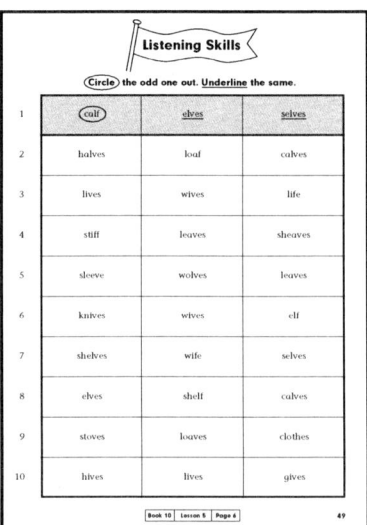

The words require some careful thought, as visual recognition does not always ensure that the phonic presentation matches. This particular exercise is challenging and stimulating for the student with specific learning difficulties.

Golden Teaching Tips

- Ensure that the student follows the directions given at the top of the page.
- To create a further challenge for students who need to develop their auditory perceptive skills, this activity should be presented orally.
- Encourage the student to underline the specific letters which display the 'same' sound.

Page 7 Cloze Procedure (Sentence Completion)

Skill Aim   *Comprehension and Writing*

Summary

Here the student needs to complete a number of sentences by selecting the correct word from the base of the page.

The student reads for meaning and grammar and neatly writes the correct word in the space. This ensures *comprehension* of the appropriate options and provides further *writing* experience.

The page contains a few illustrations which provide an indication of the appropriate location for the words, if needed. Although some words will fit in more than one sentence, there will be only one solution for the page as a whole. It is therefore essential that the student studies the sentences carefully before jumping to any conclusions!

Golden Teaching Tips

- Watch out for capital letters – these are a clue to word positions.
- Commission further illustrations from the student to confirm understanding.
- Encourage use of strategy: select easier choices first, and tick them off at the bottom of the page.

Page 8 Wordsearch

Skill Aims   *Visual Scanning   Letter Sequence*

Summary

This box grid measures ten squares across by eleven down and has been filled with letters. At the bottom of the page are found between ten and eighteen words in structure and based on the lesson topic. These need to be 'found' in the grid above by *visual scanning*. Words have been hidden horizontally forwards, vertically and diagonally downwards. No words are written backwards. Correct *letter sequence* is important.

Golden Teaching Tips

- Highlight words in the grid.
- Highlight the target words at the bottom of the page when they have been found in the grid.
- Strategy – look in the grid for clues like capital letters or the first letters of target words. Anchor the target word by tracing around the first letter in the grid, thereby looking for the next letter in that word.
- There may be additional words hidden in the grid which are not presented in the box of words under the Wordsearch. Finding such extra words can raise the confidence and self-esteem of the student.

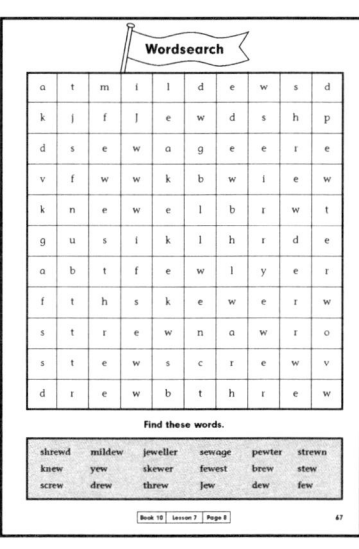

Lifeboat Programme Structure

Book 1	Lesson 1	Alphabet Sequencing
	Lesson 2	Consonants
	Lesson 3	Vowels
	Lesson 4	i
	Lesson 5	i n p s t
	Lesson 6	a
	Lesson 7	b d
	Lesson 8	sn sp st
	Lesson 9	-nd -nt
	Lesson 10	Review and Post-test
Book 2	Lesson 1	e
	Lesson 2	Open and Closed Syllables
	Lesson 3	k
	Lesson 4	Compound Words
	Lesson 5	vc/cv Syllable Breakdown
	Lesson 6	One Syllable Two Syllables
	Lesson 7	o and u
	Lesson 8	-ck
	Lesson 9	br cr dr fr gr pr tr
	Lesson 10	Review and Post-test
Book 3	Lesson 1	-ick -ic
	Lesson 2	scr spr str
	Lesson 3	i-e
	Lesson 4	bl cl fl gl pl sl spl
	Lesson 5	al -all
	Lesson 6	Vowel -y
	Lesson 7	-ff -ll -ss
	Lesson 8	Suffixes -est -less -ly -ness
	Lesson 9	Syllable Division vc/cv v̄/cv
	Lesson 10	Review and Post-test
Book 4	Lesson 1	a-e
	Lesson 2	e-e
	Lesson 3	fl fr gl gr
	Lesson 4	o-e
	Lesson 5	-ng -nk -ing
	Lesson 6	-are -ire -ore
	Lesson 7	u-e
	Lesson 8	sc sk sm sw
	Lesson 9	-lb -lf -lk -lt -mp -ct -ft -xt
	Lesson 10	Review and Post-test

This chart shows the detailed structure of the Lifeboat programme.

The student undertaking the complete programme progresses sequentially through Lessons 1 to 10 in each of the Books 1 to 8. This provides a cumulative, comprehensive knowledge of the essential constituents of the English language.

The lessons in Books 9 and 10 act as a supplement to the main programme. They are particularly suitable for work with the class or group as a whole.

When used with the main programme of Books 1 to 8, the lessons in Books 9 and 10 should ideally be integrated with those of Books 4 to 7 at the points which are indicated in the chart.

Book 10, Lesson 10 is the final Review for the complete Lifeboat scheme.

Book 9

Doubling Letters	Lesson 1
Magic 'e' Vowel Review	Lesson 2
-zz -ze -se -s (z) Sound	Lesson 3
'H' Brothers ch sh th	Lesson 4
Days and Months	Lesson 5
Numbers	Lesson 6
Contractions	Lesson 7
Plural -es	Lesson 8
Suffix Drop 'e'	Lesson 9
Prefixes	Lesson 10

	Lesson 1	**Suffix Drop 'y'**			
			qu squ -que	Lesson 1	**Book 5**
			ee oo	Lesson 2	
			ar er or	Lesson 3	
			-ed	Lesson 4	
			-ay	Lesson 5	
			-ce -se -nce	Lesson 6	
			Soft 'c' (s) Sound	Lesson 7	
	Lesson 2	**Soft 'g' (j) Sound**	**-ge -dge -age**	Lesson 8	
			ch -tch	Lesson 9	
			Review and Post-test	Lesson 10	
			-ble -dle -gle -ple -tle -zle	Lesson 1	**Book 6**
			ea ee	Lesson 2	
			ai -ain	Lesson 3	
			ir	Lesson 4	
			oa	Lesson 5	
	Lesson 3	**ou (ow) Sound**			
			-ow	Lesson 6	
Book 10	Lesson 4	**Silent Letters**			
	Lesson 5	**Change f/fe to -ves**			
			igh	Lesson 7	
	Lesson 6	**ur**			
			au -aw	Lesson 8	
	Lesson 7	**-ew**			
			-tion	Lesson 9	
			Review and Post-test	Lesson 10	
	Lesson 8	**ie**			
			Odd Plurals Plural Review	Lesson 1	**Book 7**
			Wild Old Words	Lesson 2	
	Lesson 9	**ei**			
			ph -gh (f) Sound	Lesson 3	
			oi -oy	Lesson 4	
			ear	Lesson 5	
			wh 'H' Brothers Review	Lesson 6	
			Schwa	Lesson 7	
			ch (3 Sounds)	Lesson 8	
			-an -en -ant -ent -ancy -ency	Lesson 9	
			Review and Post-test	Lesson 10	
			ou (7 Sounds)	Lesson 1	**Book 8**
			-ey	Lesson 2	
			-ure -ture	Lesson 3	
			-al -el	Lesson 4	
			-us -ous -ious	Lesson 5	
			-sion	Lesson 6	
			-ar -or (er) Sound	Lesson 7	
			-cian	Lesson 8	
			ci si ti xi	Lesson 9	
			Review and Post-test	Lesson 10	
	Lesson 10	**Review of Whole Scheme**			

Lifeboat Assessment 1

Name: ....
Date: ....

Book 1	it	pin	sat	bit	had
	spin	snap	band	mint	stand

Book 2	step	he	kid	wigwam	catkin
	log	bun	neck	track	print

Book 3	kick	fabric	scrub	time	clock
	hall	lucky	hill	costly	pony

Book 4	plane	swede	flake	slope	spring
	backfire	cube	scare	bulb	lamp

Book 9	hopping	stampede	capsize	chunk	February
	million	you're	buzzes	driving	express

Book 5	quake	football	spark	drilled	runway
	mice	commence	delicacy	bridge	sketched

Book 6	angle	already	certain	birthplace	coaching
	elbow	fright	exhausting	yawn	expectation

Book 7	children	grinding	emphatic	asteroid	enjoy
	earthquake	whisper	alphabet	chemistry	vacancy

Book 10	ladies	generated	bounced	combing	shelves
	windsurf	mildew	shield	reindeer	virtuously

Book 8	young	pricey	literature	angel	enormous
	suspension	accelerator	obstetrician	ambitious	brochure

NOTES

Lifeboat Assessment 2

Name: ....

Date: ....

Book 1	in	sit	tap	hid	bat
	snip	span	sand	hint	hand

Book 2	spend	be	kit	napkin	Batman
	cod	run	back	crab	trend

Book 3	tick	public	sprint	lifeline	plug
	wall	sticky	cliff	sickness	unity

Book 4	snake	eve	frost	globe	blink
	snore	flute	skyline	lift	belt

Book 9	foggy	strike	bronze	splash	Wednesday
	thousand	we're	publishes	hoping	demagnetize

Book 5	square	monsoon	morning	hissed	spray
	face	chance	centigrade	bandage	stretch

Book 6	indigestible	cleanliness	captain	firmly	lifeboat
	window	light	authentic	prawn	fraction

Book 7	geese	kindness	decipher	toiletries	enjoyment
	earlier	whether	topography	echo	indignant

Book 10	ponies	germinate	foreground	wrist	knives
	Thursday	knew	brief	receive	corduroy

Book 8	group	survey	temperature	squirrel	felicitous
	propulsion	lunar	politician	anxiously	conscientiously

NOTES

Lifeboat Record Chart

Name: ....

Assessment 1 Date: .... Reading/Spelling.   Assessment 2 Date: .... Reading/Spelling.

	1	2	3	4	5
Book 1	Alphabet Sequencing	Consonants	Vowels	i	i n p s t
	6 a	7 b d	8 sn sp st	9 -nd -nt	10 Review and Post-test
Book 2	1 e	2 Open and Closed Syllables	3 k	4 Compound Words	5 vc / cv Syllable Breakdown
	6 One Syllable Two Syllables	7 o and u	8 -ck	9 br cr dr fr gr pr tr	10 Review and Post-test
Book 3	1 -ick -ic	2 scr spr str	3 i-e	4 bl cl fl gl pl sl spl	5 al -all
	6 Vowel -y	7 -ff -ll -ss	8 Suffixes -est -less -ly -ness	9 Syllable Division vc / cv v̄ / cv	10 Review and Post-test
Book 4	1 a-e	2 e-e	3 fl fr gl gr	4 o-e	5 -ng -nk -ing
Book 9	*1 Doubling Letters*	6 -are -ire -ore	7 u-e	*2 Magic 'e' Vowel Review*	8 sc sk sm sw
	3 -zz -ze -se -s (z) Sound	*4 'H' Brothers ch sh th*	9 -lb -lf -lk -lt -mp -ct -ft xt	*5 Days and Months*	*6 Numbers*
	7 Contractions	10 Review and Post-test	*8 Plural -es*	*9 Suffix Drop 'e'*	*10 Prefixes*
Book 10	1 **Suffix Drop 'y'**	1 qu squ -que	2 ee oo	3 ar er or	4 -ed
Book 5	5 -ay	6 -ce -se -nce	7 Soft 'c' (s) Sound	8 -ge -dge -age	**2 Soft 'g' (j) Sound**
	9 ch -tch	10 Review and Post-test			
Book 6	1 -ble -dle -gle -ple -tle -zle	2 ea ee	3 ai -ain	4 ir	5 oa
	3 ou (ow) Sound	6 -ow	**4 Silent Letters**	**5 Change f / fe to -ves**	7 igh
	6 ur	8 au -aw	**7 -ew**	9 -tion	10 Review and Post-test
Book 7	**8 ie**	1 Odd Plurals Plural Review	2 Wild Old Words	**9 ei**	3 ph -gh (f) Sound
	4 oi -oy	5 ear	6 wh 'H' Brothers Review	7 Schwa	8 ch (3 Sounds)
	9 -an -en -ant -ent -ancy ency	10 Review and Post-test			
Book 8	1 ou (7 Sounds)	2 -ey	3 -ure -ture	4 -al -el	5 -us -ous -ious
	6 -sion	7 -ar -or (er) Sound	8 -cian	9 ci si ti xi	10 Review and Post-test
	10 Review of Whole Scheme	Book 9 Lessons are shown in	*bold italicised text*		
		Book 10 Lessons are shown in	**bold text**		

Student Progress Chart

Name: ....

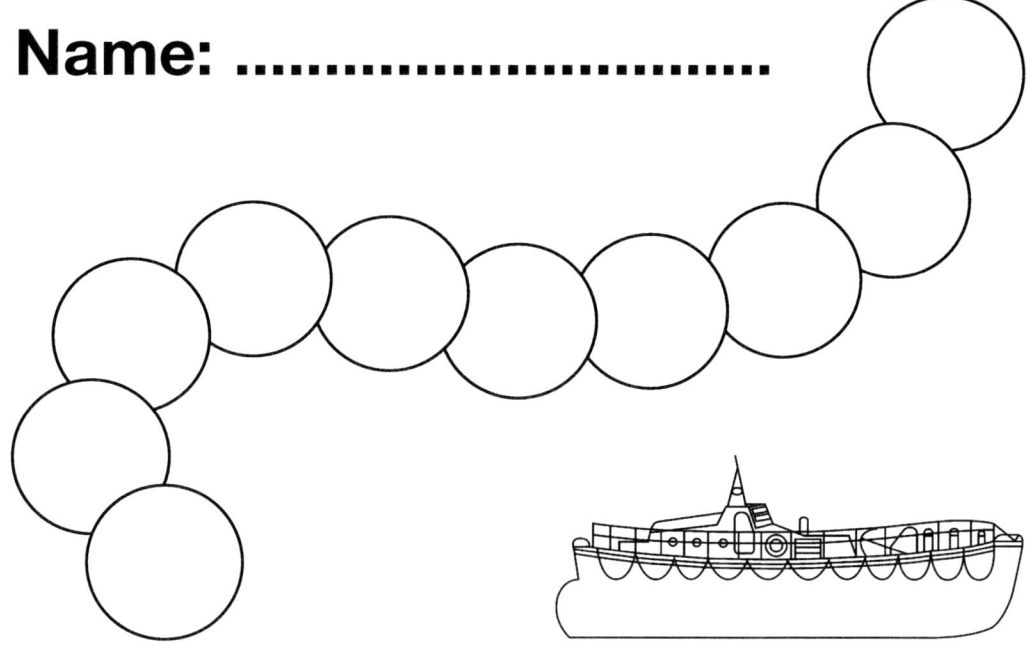

Certificate of Achievement

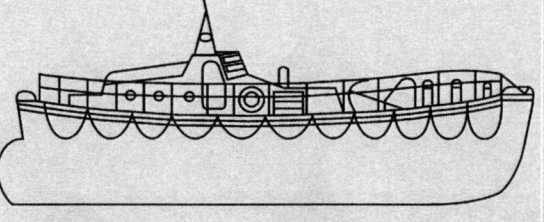

....

has completed

Lifeboat Book ......

Launch the Lifeboat to Read and Spell

Lesson Notes to Book 1

This foundation book is a vital experience for the beginner. Lessons 1 to 3 are introductory with the structured programme starting in Lesson 4. Breaking language up in to small manageable steps, as found in Book 1, is essential for opening the door to literacy for the student.

Lesson 1   Alphabet Sequencing
The alphabet sequence has been presented here in four parts, matching the four quartiles of a dictionary:

         a - d   e - m   n - r   s - z

Here are the basic alphabet skills needed for the student's career: from Shakespeare to Internet.

Lesson 2   Consonants
Here the pupil encounters consonant sounds and where consonants come in the alphabet. Cursive handwriting is introduced straight away. The use of pure sounds is encouraged.

Lesson 3   Vowels
This lesson presents the order of the vowels in the alphabet, short vowel sounds and cursive handwriting. [*Early word*: 'vowels'.]

Lesson 4   i
This lesson marks the start of the Lifeboat programme. Short 'i' is studied through visual, auditory and kinaesthetic learning channels. Lower case and capital letters are to be matched as well as learning and reviewing the alphabet order **a b c d e f g h i**.

Lesson 5   i n p s t
From this point, the student can launch off successfully into reading and spelling words that include the letters **i n p s t**. This is a key lesson to give the complete beginner a feeling of achievement. Exercises are designed to move the student gradually into the future structure of Lifeboat. Plural 's' is included; 's' can make two sounds: (s), or (z) as on the end of 'is'. In the Lifeboat scheme, the use of brackets, as in (z), denotes 'sound of'. [*Sight words*: 'of', 'do'. *Early words*: 'the', 'my', 'at', 'as', 'we', 'me', 'go', 'am', 'by'.]

Lesson 6   a
The format used for most of the Lifeboat scheme is introduced in this lesson. It is designed to encourage independent study (see Teaching Guide pages 10 to 13). Only **i n p s t** and **a** (and 'the') are used for reading words and dictation. In this lesson **a** makes the short sound (ă). When 's' is on the end of a word after an 'n', it makes the sound (z) as in 'spins'. When 's' is on the end of a word after a 'p' or a 't', it makes the sound (s) as in 'snaps' and 'sits'. Notice how the strength of the sound 't' has been reduced in the word 'sits'. Some of these letters are in blends, which will be covered in greater detail in Lesson 8.

Lesson 7   b d
These two letters are commonly confused. For the tracking exercise, **b** could be tracked in one colour and **d** in another. The student could place their hands as shown in the illustration to make the word 'bed', as a strategy to help them work at **b** and **d**. Students work with the sound these letters make and do cursive handwriting for them.

Lesson 8   sn sp st
Here, the first consonant blends are studied in depth. All these letters have been covered in Lesson 5. The reading and spelling elements are carefully in structure, including only letters covered from Lesson 4 onwards. Capital letters feature for names and for the start of a sentence. When 's' is on the end of a word after a 'b', it makes the sound (z) as in 'stabs'. It says (z) in 'as'. The consonant **h** has also been included. In Lesson 8, the vowels 'a' and 'i' appear with their long sound as words in their own right ('a' and 'I').

Lesson 9   -nd -nt

This is the first lesson dedicated to end blends, again within the structure of letters covered from Lesson 4 onwards. As an example of an **-nt** ending, the word 'dint' is used in this lesson. Although less frequently used than 'dent', the meaning is identical. The dash in front of the **-nd** and **-nt** indicates that these letters are on the end of the word. This is the reason for the dash ' **-** ' throughout the Lifeboat programme. [*Early word*: 'y<u>ou</u>'.]

Lesson 10   Review and Post-test

This is a lesson that pulls together reading and spelling for **i n p s t a b d** and **h** from which the blends **sn sp st -nd -nt** can be composed.

Lesson 1

Alphabet Sequencing

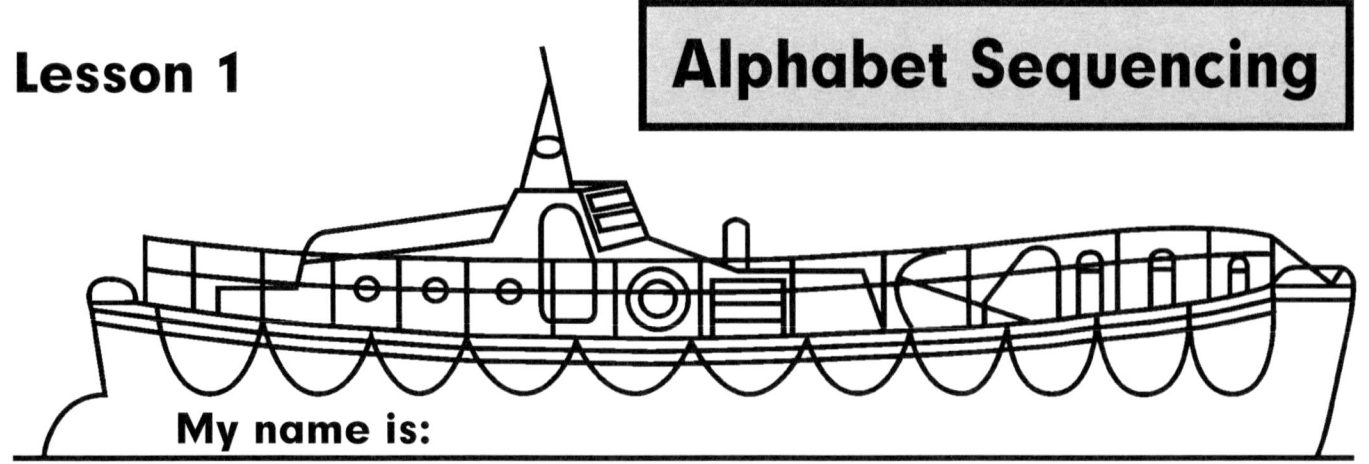

My name is:

The Alphabet Maze

Follow the alphabet order: a b c d

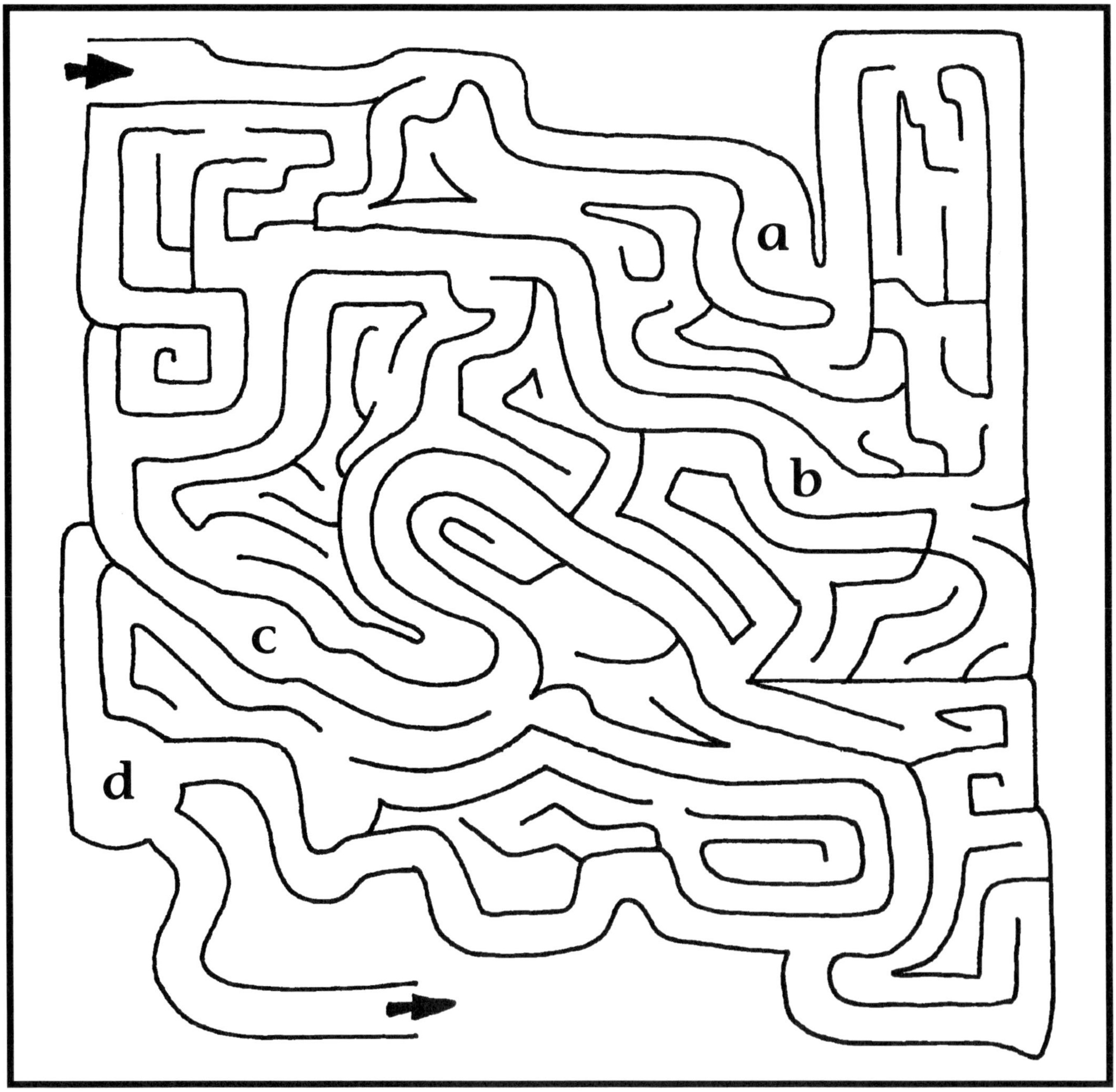

Follow the alphabet order: e f g h i j k l m

Follow the alphabet order: n o p q r

Follow the alphabet order: s t u v w x y z

Start at a and draw a line to the next letter in the alphabet.

a b

c

d

e

k

f g

j

h

l

i

m

Start at n and draw a line to the next letter in the alphabet.

n

r

o   p

x

q

s   v

w

t   u

y   z

Track for the alphabet.

| a | b | c | d | e | f | g | h | i | j | k | l | m |
| n | o | p | q | r | s | t | u | v | w | x | y | z |

c d ⓐ f e r n b v d e s a g b

n c j k l e d s g d e f m q y

u r f s c x g m w q r h g i f

c x z b d s j m k h r e w q

t h l b n f k w q p o r m n

k r e w s c x b m o m t p f

v b n q y t r n m k l v b e

r t s m z k n m l o p t h d

s c v n w u k l n m b c s x

b e w g v g t u w c n h k l

p y x w u k q d f r b g t h

j u y g b w s d c z g h j l

Join the dots in the order of the alphabet: a b c d...

Fill in the missing letters in the alphabet.

a b __ d e __ g h i __ k l m

n o __ q r s __ u v __ __ y z

Lesson 2

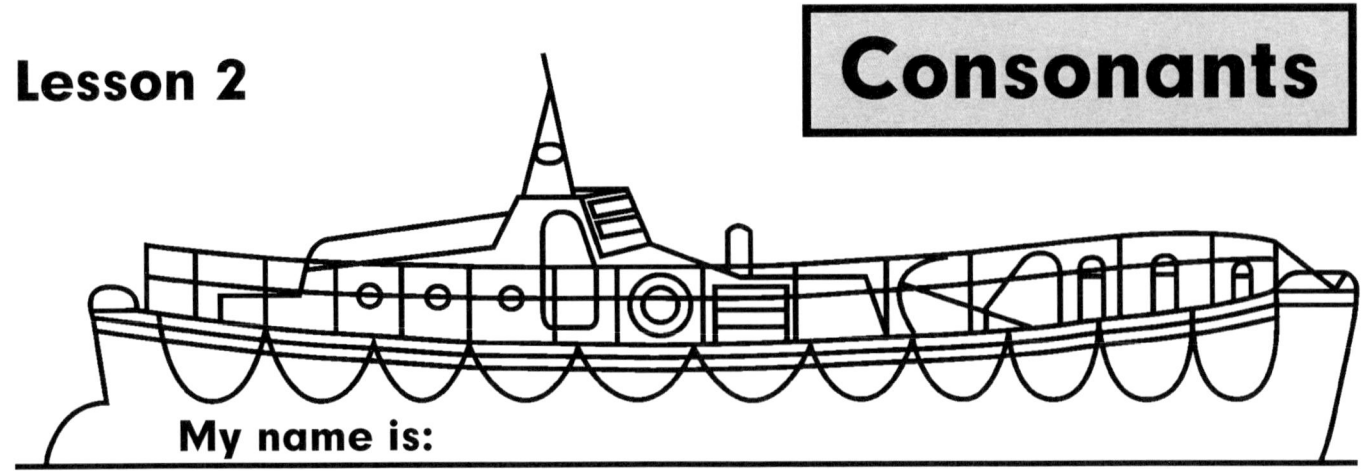

My name is:

Consonants

These are the consonants:

__ b c d __ f g h __ j k l m
n __ p q r s t __ v w x y z

Fill in the missing letters. Write the first letter of the picture in the box.

a _b_ c __ e f __ __ i j k

| d | | | |

__ k l __ n o p __ r __ t

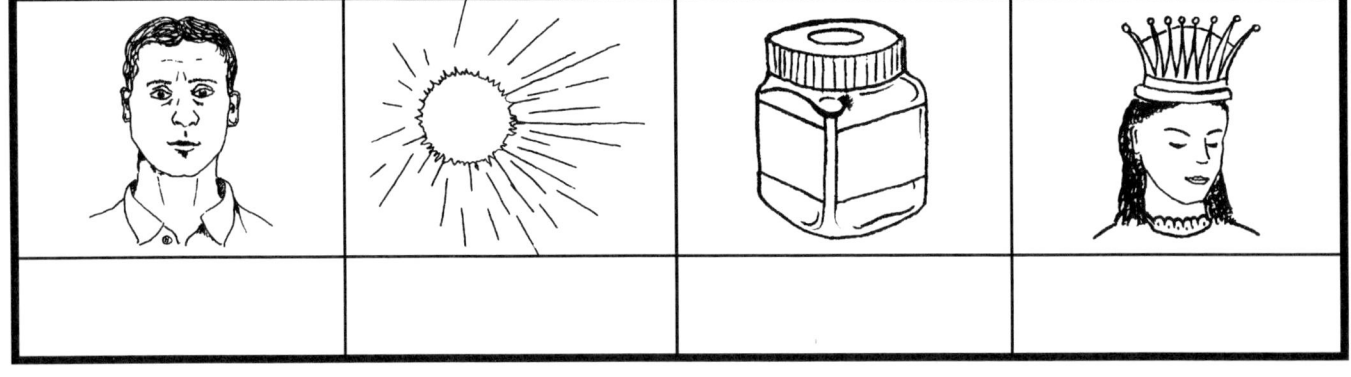

p q _ s t _ v _ x _ z

r _ t u _ w _ y _

Fill in the missing letters.

a b c d e f _ _ i j k l _ n
o p _ r s t u _ _ x _ _

What is the first letter?

Listen to the first sound and circle the picture that starts with the same sound.

Book 1 | Lesson 2 | Page 3

Listen to the last sound and circle the picture that ends with the same sound.

These are the consonants:

_ b c d _ f g h _ _ j k l m
n _ p q r s t _ v w x y z

Choose the first letter.

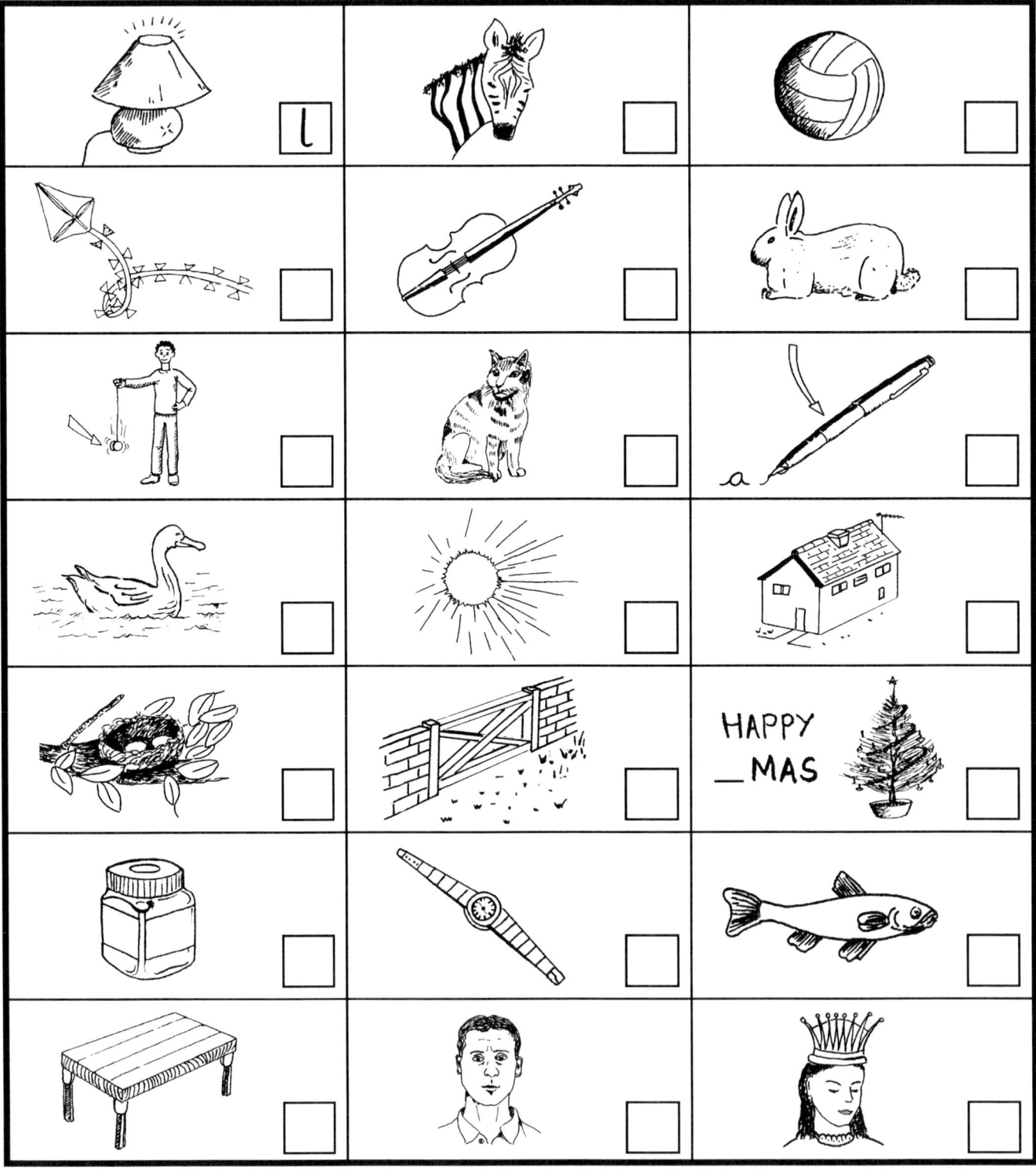

These are the consonants:

_ b c d _ f g h _ j k l m
n _ p q r s t _ v w x y z

Choose the last letter.

Joined Handwriting

r

g

h

z

Trace:

j m q r w x y

Letter Strings

rghz

jmqv

wxy

myvr

Write any of these letters with eyes closed!

Lesson 3

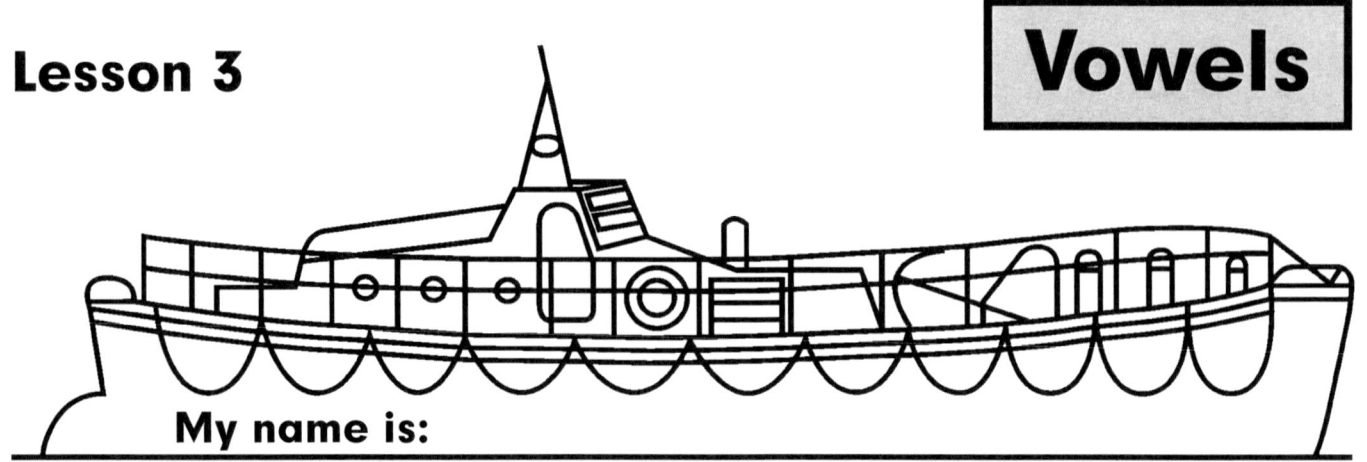

My name is:

Track for the vowels in the order: a e i o u

```
c  d  (a) f  (e) r  n  b  v  d  (i) s  a  g  b  n
c  j  k  l  o  d  s  g  d  u  f  m  q  y  a  r
f  s  c  x  g  m  w  q  r  h  e  i  f  c  x  z
b  d  o  j  m  k  h  r  e  w  u  t  h  l  b  n
f  k  w  a  p  o  r  m  n  k  r  e  w  s  c  i
b  m  o  m  t  u  p  a  v  b  n  q  y  t  r
e  m  k  l  v  b  i  r  t  s  m  z  k  n  m  l
o  p  t  h  d  s  c  v  n  w  u  k  l  n  m
b  c  a  x  b  e  w  g  v  g  t  i  w  c  n  h
k  l  p  y  x  o  u  k  a  q  f  e  i  g  o  h
j  u  y  g  b  w  s  d  c  z  g  h  j  k
```

Circle the same letter.

a	ⓐ	d	ⓐ	b	e
e	s	c	e	e	m
i	l	i	e	i	f
o	o	g	i	p	o
u	v	u	y	z	u

Joined Handwriting

a e i o u

Join the words to the pictures.

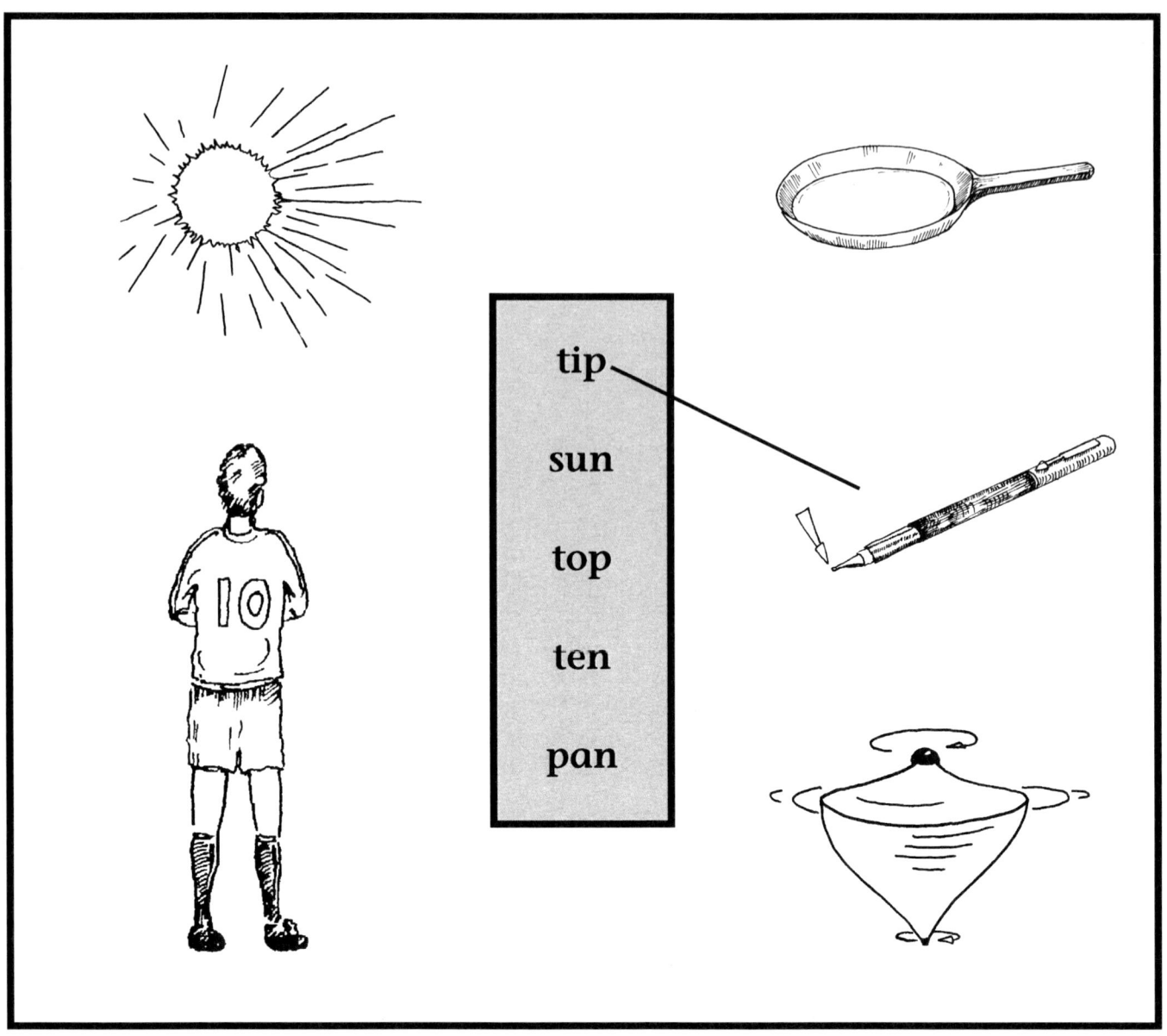

Write each word in the correct vowel box.

a	e	i	o	u
		tip		

Circle the right word.

🛏️	bad	(bed)	bid	bod	bud
🍔	ban	Ben	bin	bon	bun
👕	tan	ten	tin	ton	tun
🎩	hat	het	hit	hot	hut
🪴	pat	pet	pit	pot	put
🐟	fan	fen	fin	fon	fun
🔩	nat	net	nit	not	nut
🪵	lag	leg	lig	log	lug

Follow the vowel order – become a star student.

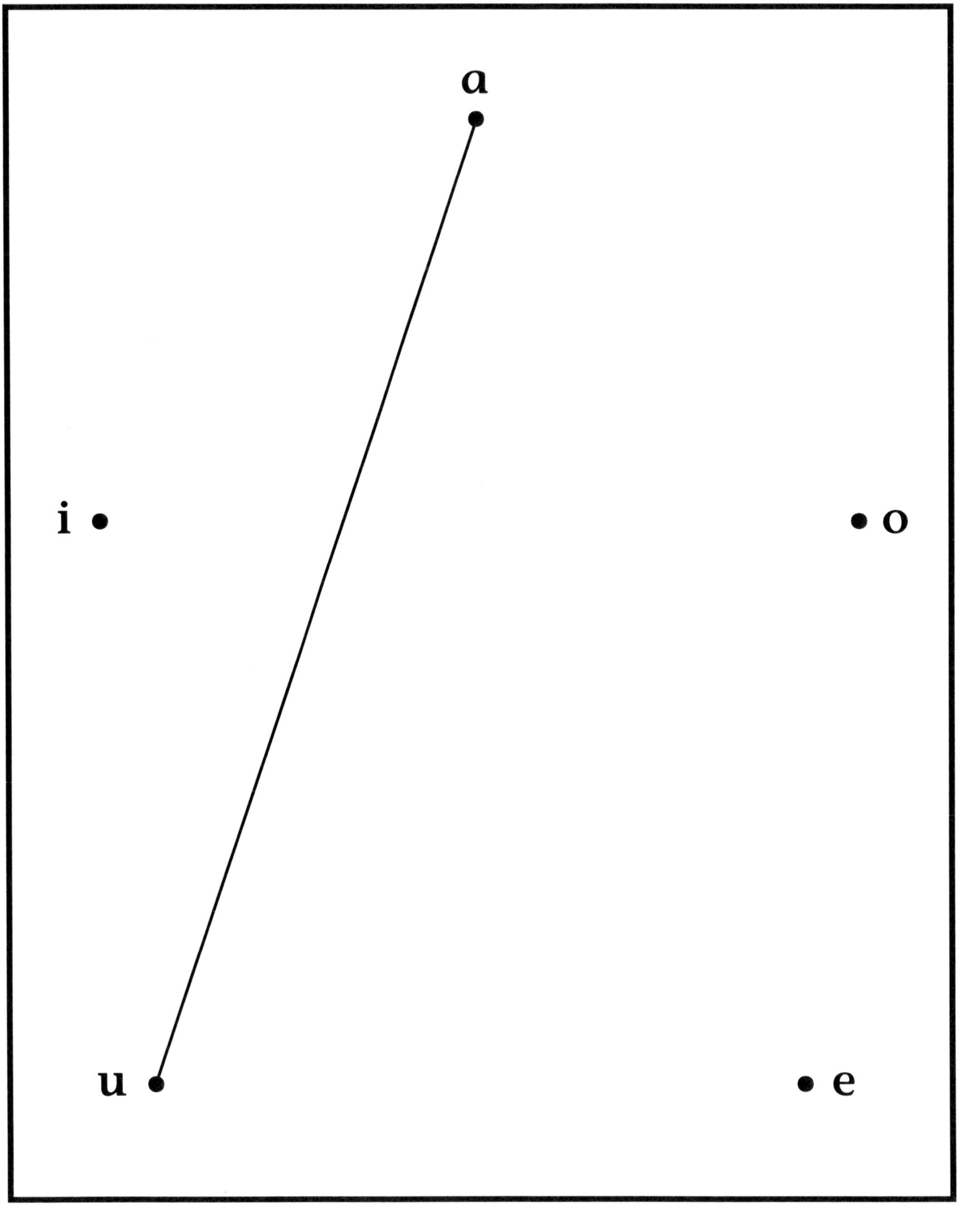

a

i •   • o

u •   • e

Dot to Dot

Follow the vowel order – can you make the word vowels?

a u a a u e a a e
 u a
e o o i i e i
 e
i i e o o u i o u u o

s w
o l
e v
v
___ ___ ___ ___ ___ ___

Joined Handwriting

close eyes

a *a*

e *e*

i *i*

Book 1 | Lesson 3 | Page 7

Joined Handwriting

close eyes

Lesson 4

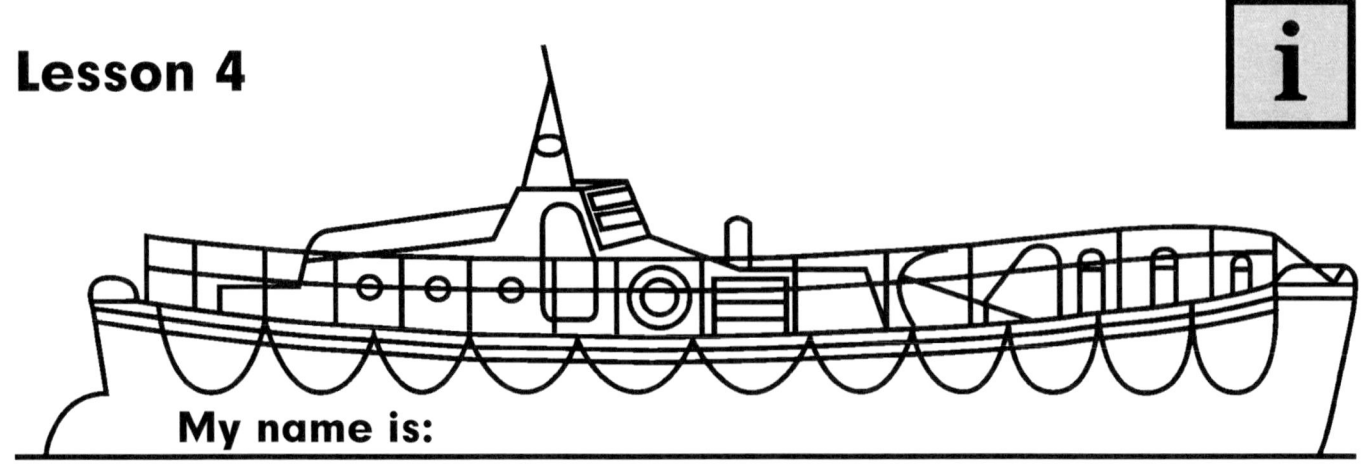

My name is:

If the first sound is (ĭ) mark *i* on it.

Book 1 | Lesson 4 | Page 1

Circle the letter i.

(i)	m	i	i	p	s
s	i	p	q	i	r
i	h	l	i	t	i
a	i	x	i	i	v
k	d	i	s	r	i
i	j	i	z	i	g
i	i	m	i	i	b
j	t	i	f	i	i

Track: i.

a	b	c	d	e	f	g	h	i	j	k	l	m
n	o	p	q	r	s	t	u	v	w	x	y	z

c d (i) f e r n b v d (i) s a g b
n i j k l e d s g i e f m i y
u r f s c x i m w q i h g i
f i x z b d s i m i h r e w
q t j l i n f k w q i o r m
n k r e w i c x b m o i t p
f i b n q y t i n m i l v b e
r t i m z i n m i o p t h d
i c v n w u k l n m b i s i
b e i g v g t u w c n h k l
i i x w u k q i f r b g t h j
i j g i w s d c z g i j k l

Listen for (ĭ) in the middle. Mark *i*.

Joined Handwriting.

close eyes

Link the word to the picture.

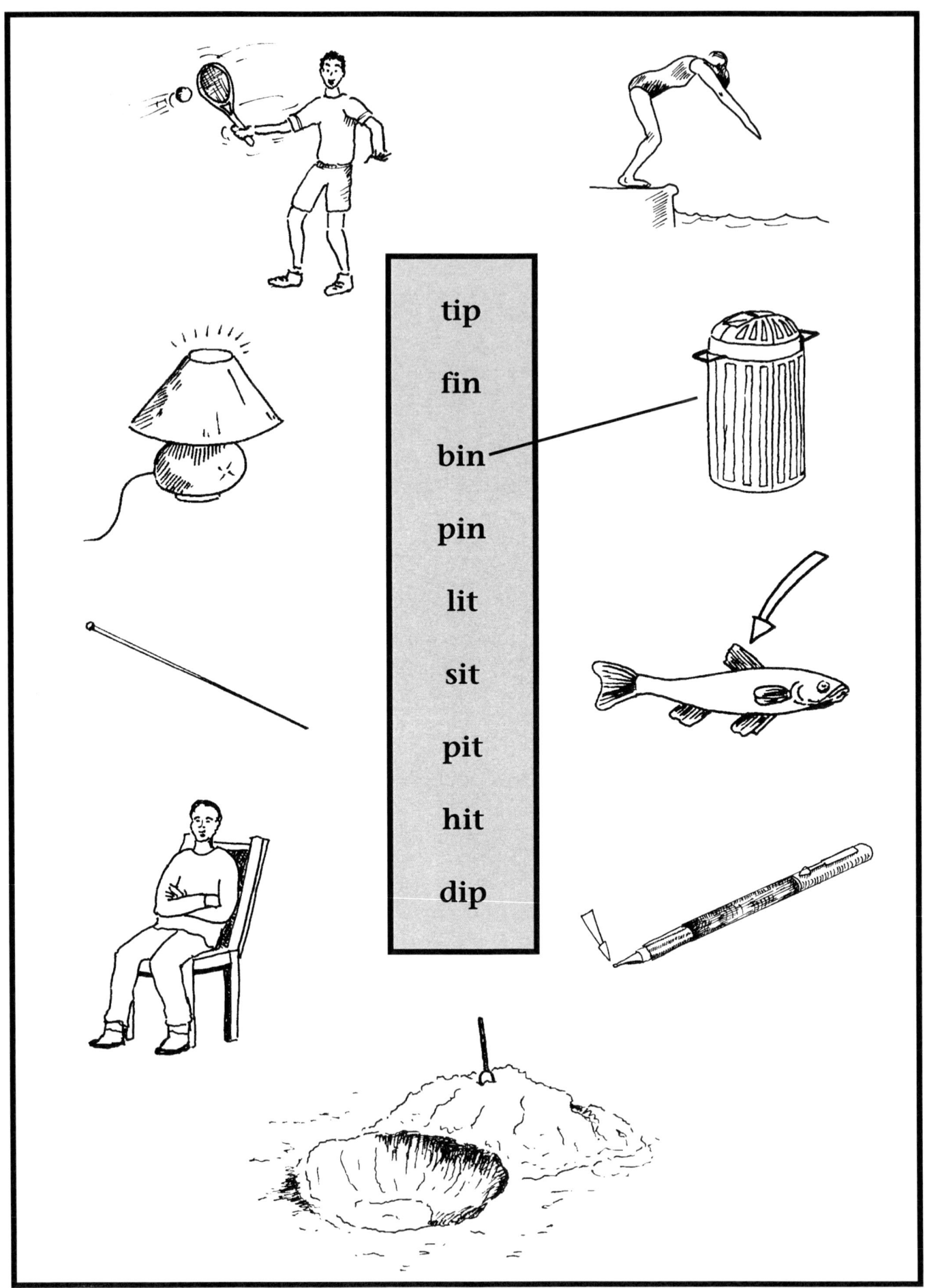

Is there an (ĭ) in these?

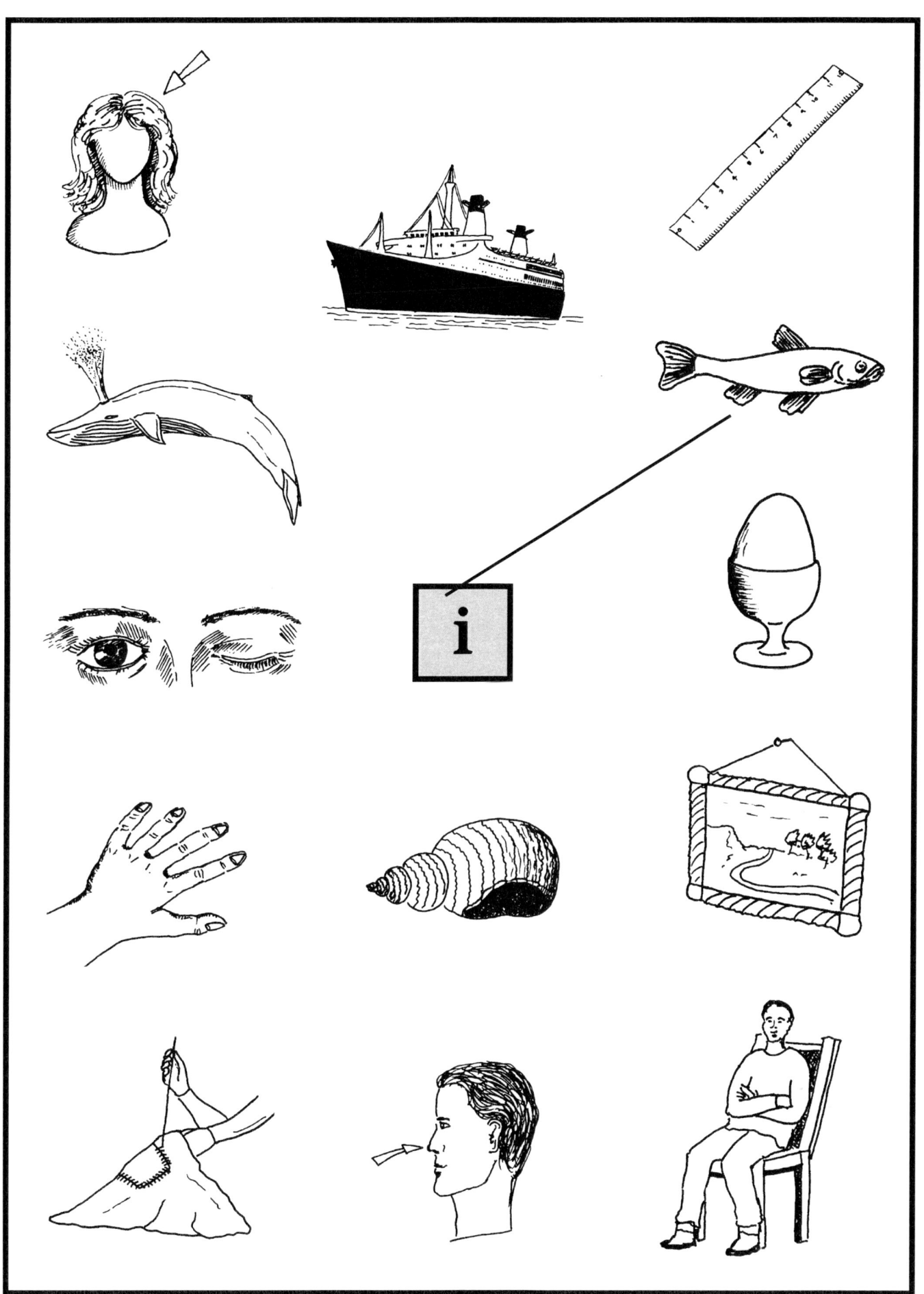

Match with the capital letters.

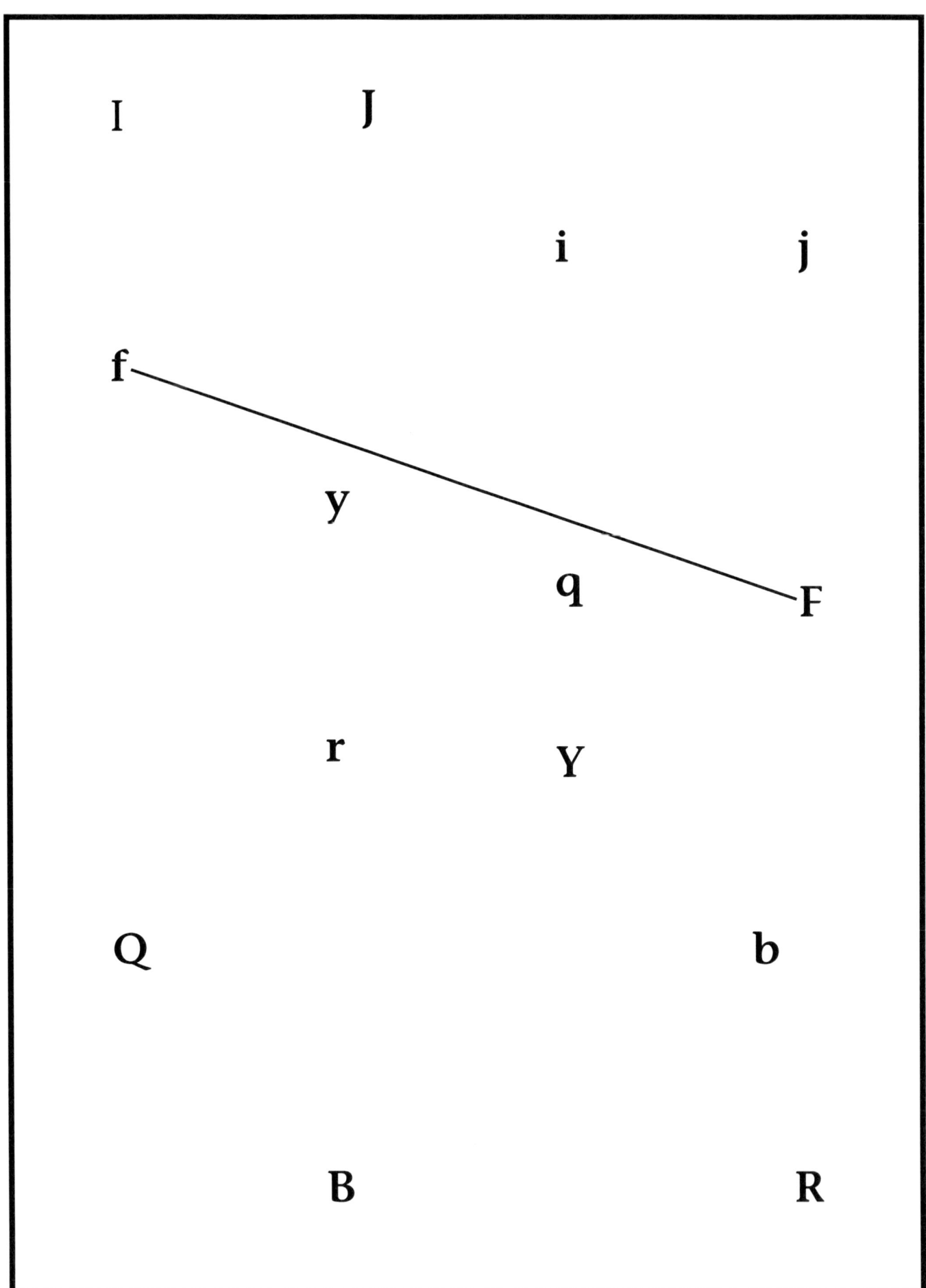

Follow the alphabet order.

a b c d e f g h i

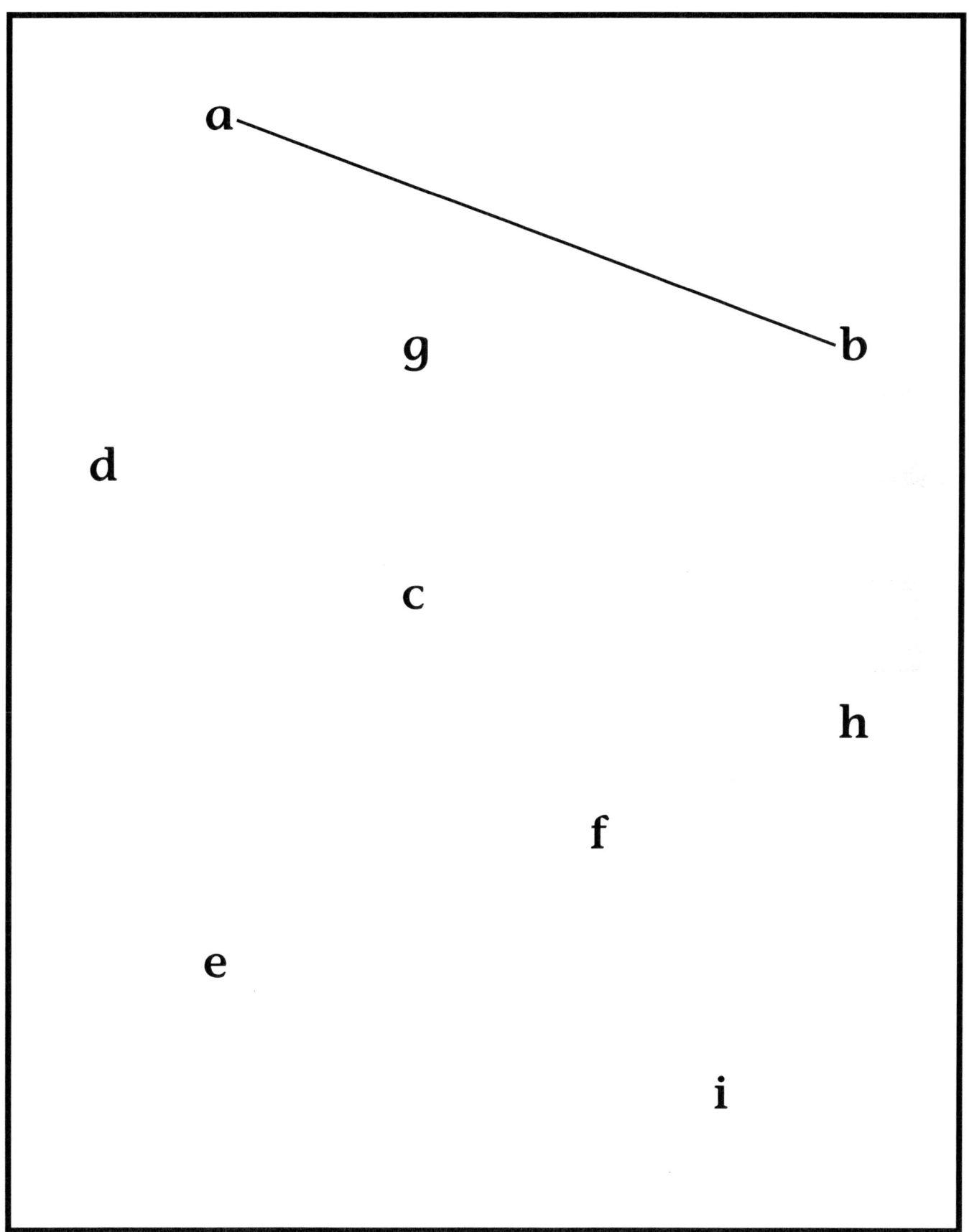

Lesson 5

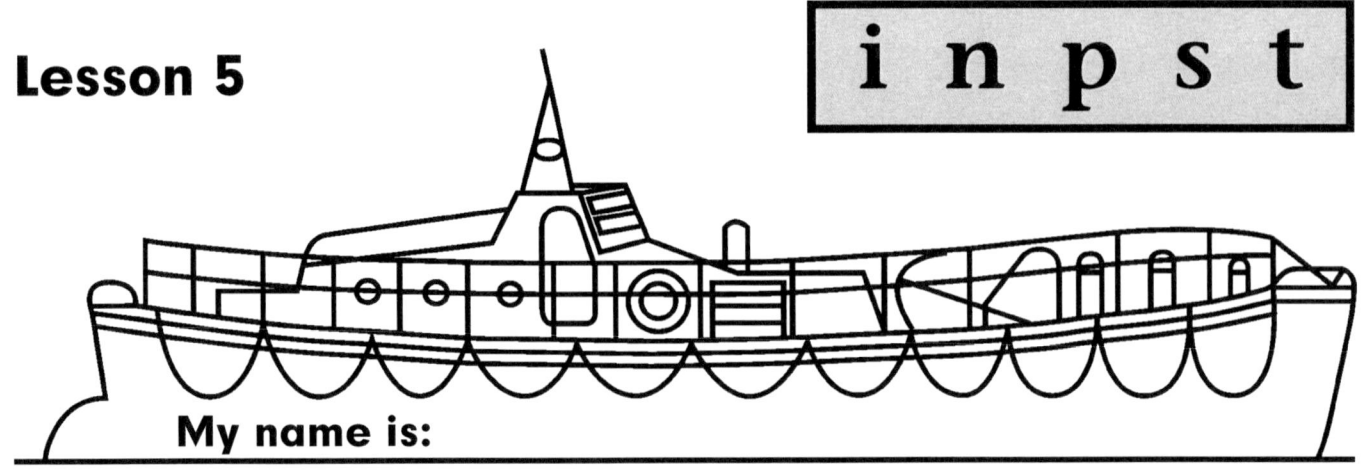

My name is:

Say (t). Cut off the sound with scissor hands.
Say (t). Feel the air on the palm of your hand.

Where do you hear (t)?
Is it at the <u>beginning</u>, <u>middle</u> or <u>end</u> of the words?

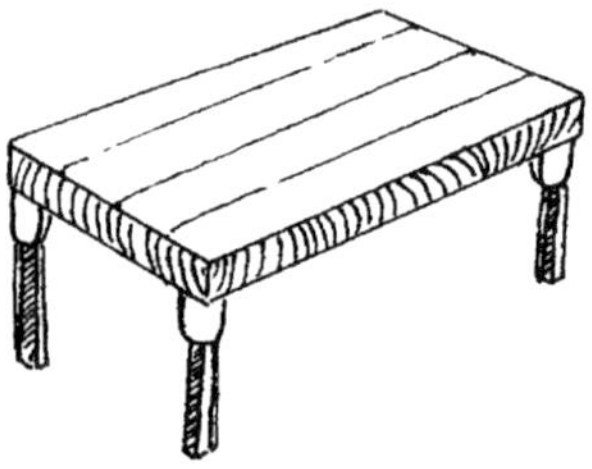

t

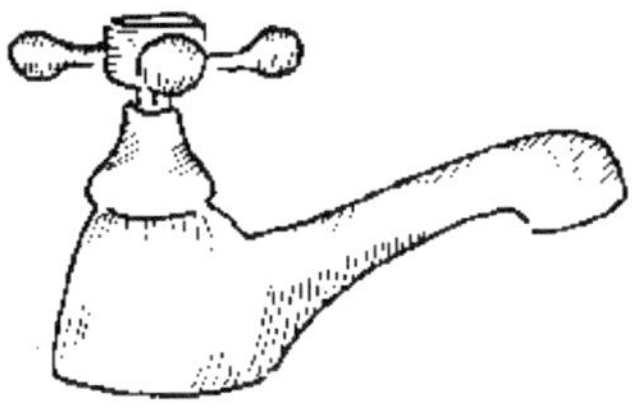

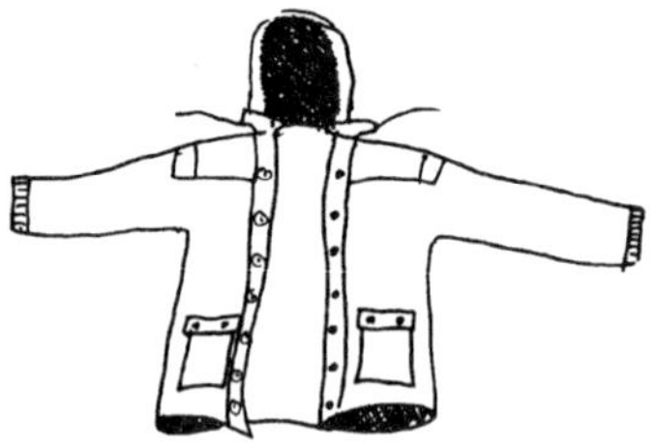

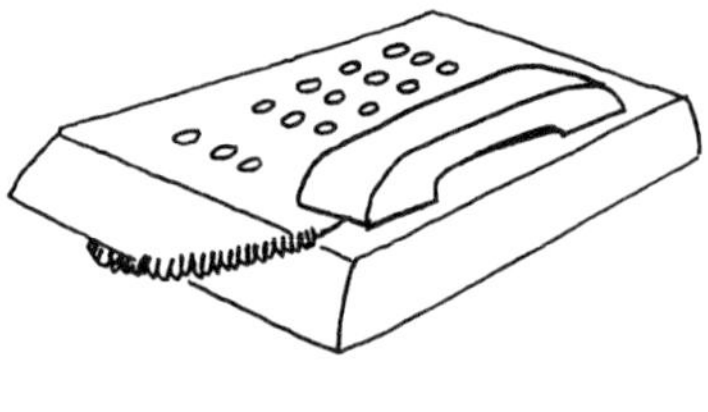

54 | Book 1 | Lesson 5 | Page 1

Track: it.

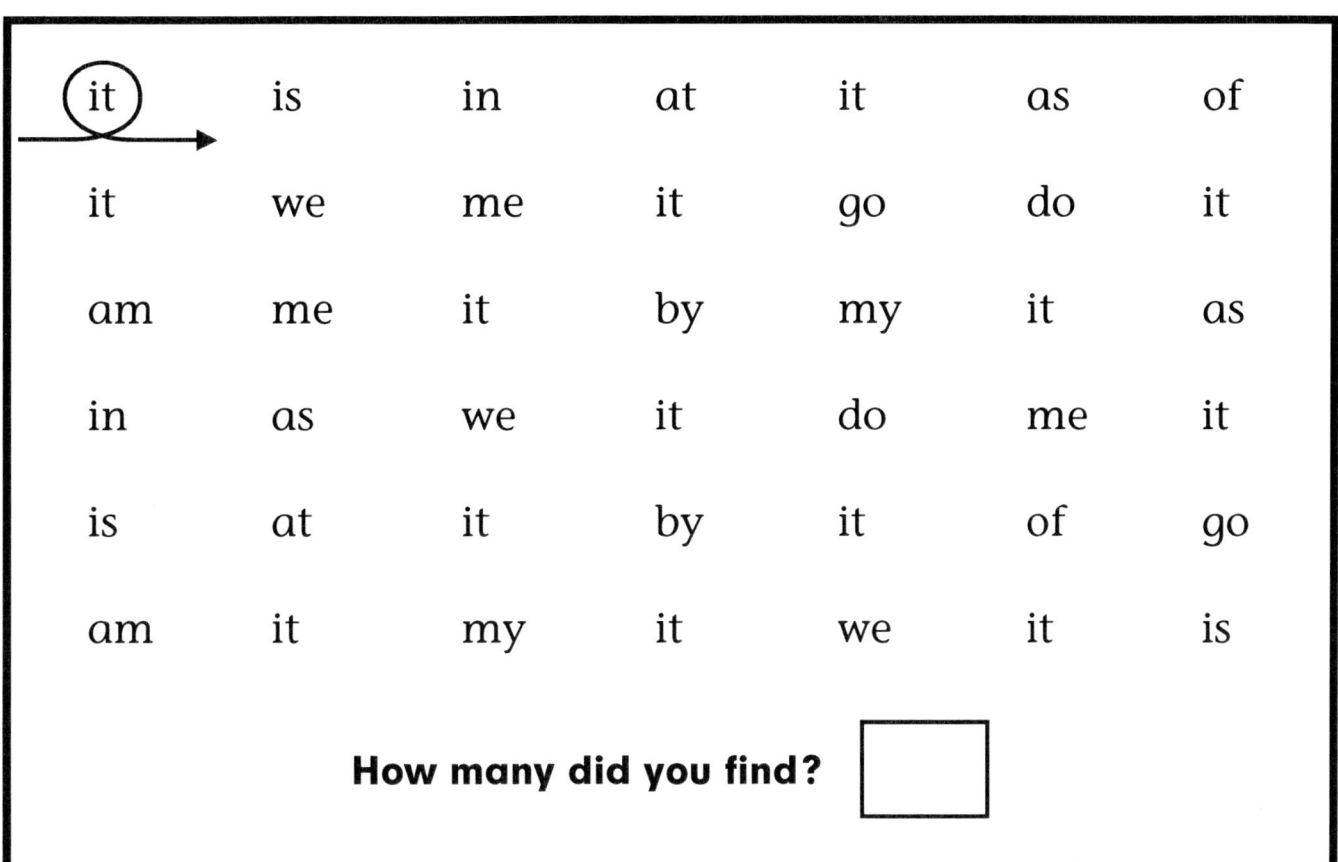

Handwriting – trace and do.

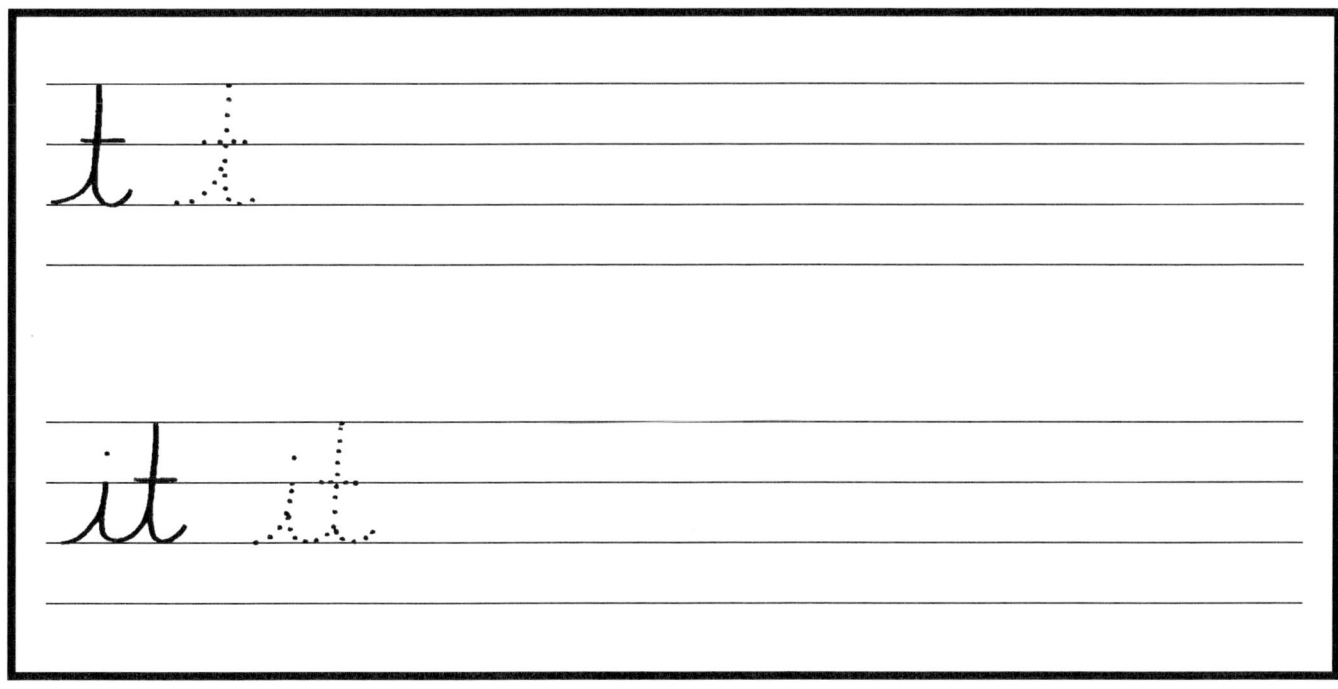

Join the word to the picture.

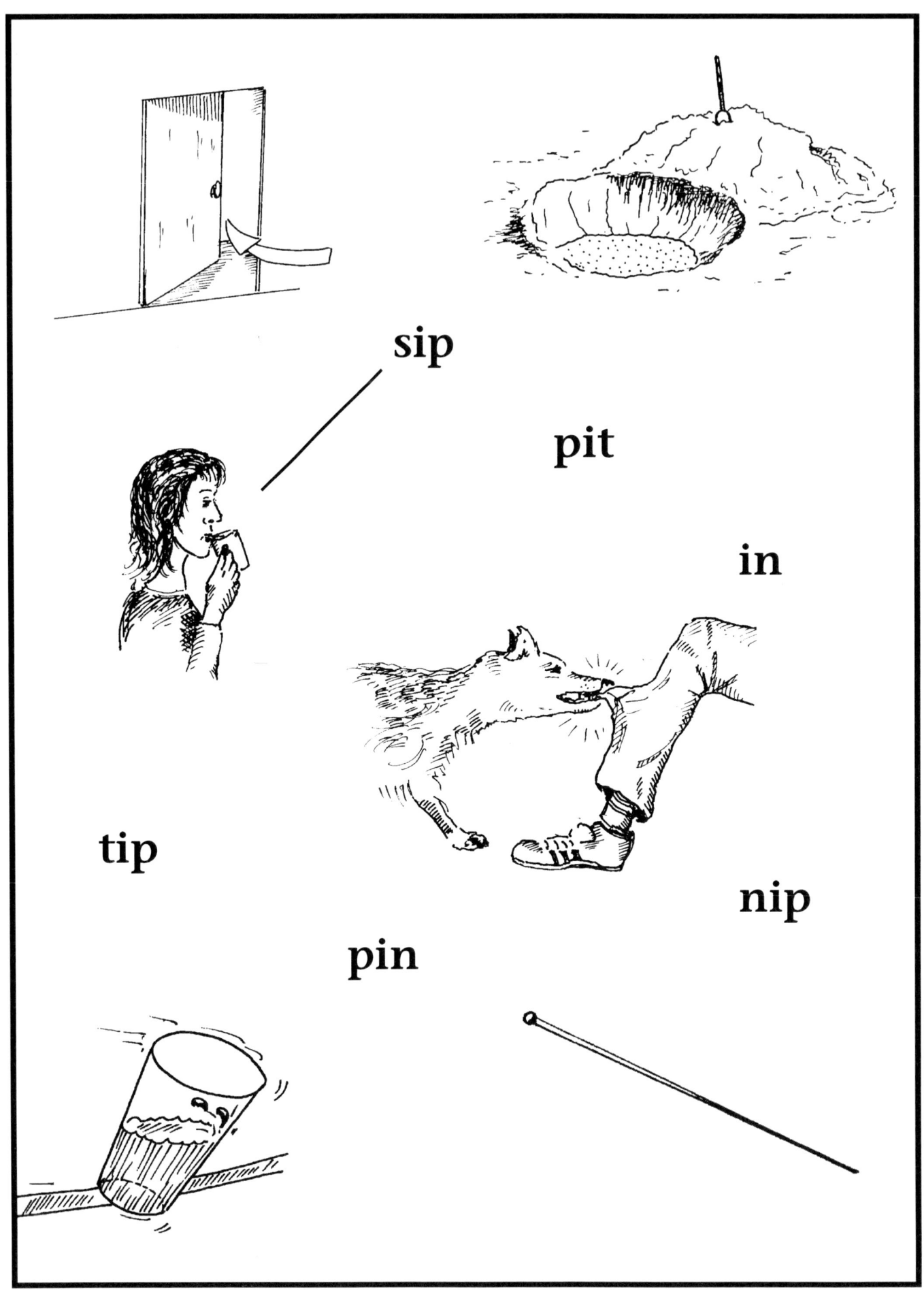

Word Match

Circle the same word.

nip	pin	(nip)	inp
sip	sit	isp	sip
pin	pin	ipn	nip
tin	nit	int	tin
pit	pit	tip	pti
tip	pit	tip	tpi
sit	its	tis	sit

Join the picture to the first letter.

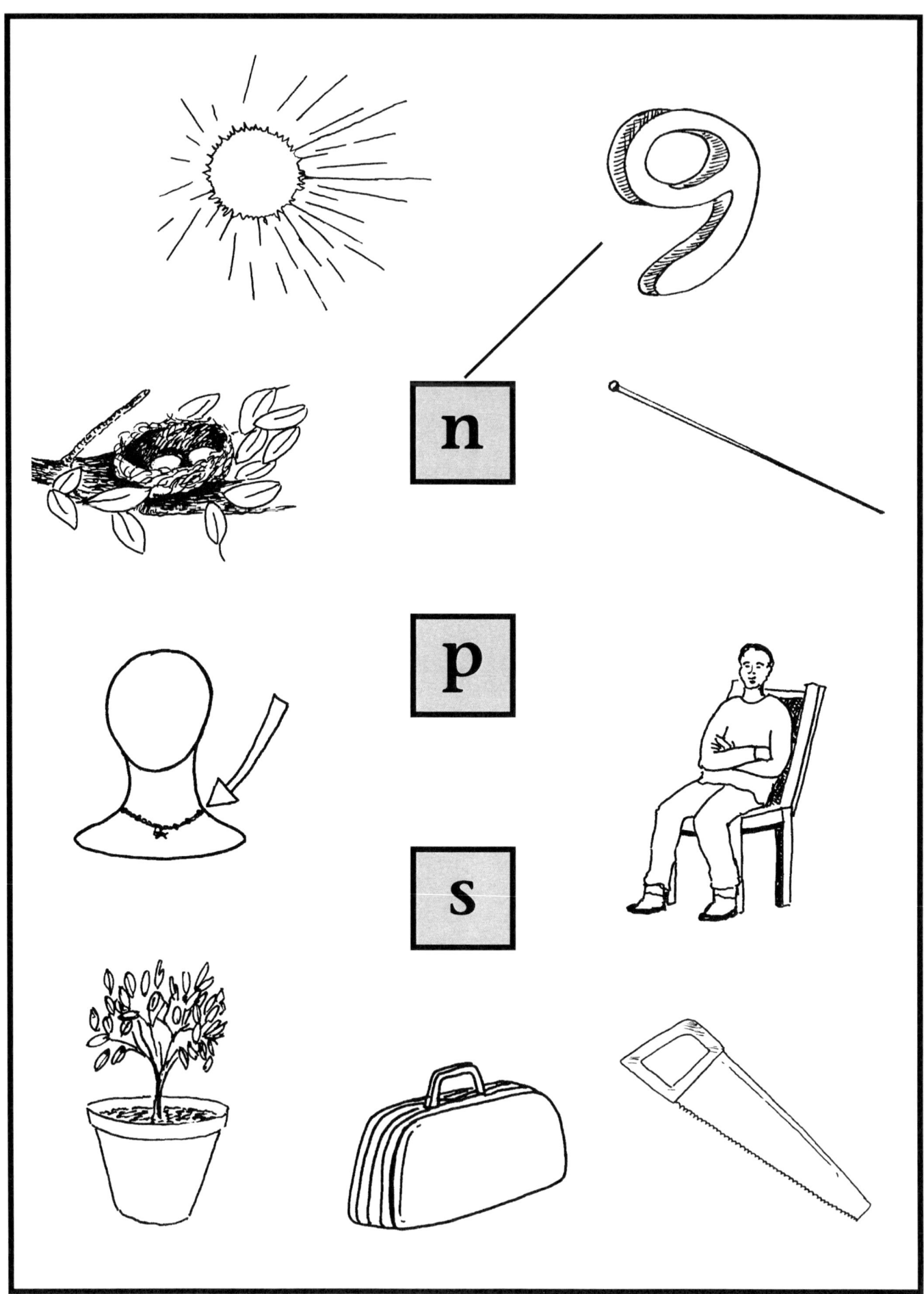

Spell and Write

Circle the letters. Write the word.

Letters	Picture	Word
(i) t (n)	(door - in)	*in*
s n / i / t p	(person sitting)	
t p / i / s n	(pin/stick)	
n s / i / t p	(biting)	
t n / i / p n	(tipping cup)	
t s / i / n p	(sipping)	

Book 1 | Lesson 5 | Page 6

Dictation or Look – Say – Cover – Write – Check

Reading and Writing.

Give help with 'the'. _____the_____ .

1 Tip the pins in the tin.

_____

What sound does S make in the word pins? ☐

2 The pin is in the tin.

_____

3 It is in the pit.

_____

4 It is in.

_____

Trace and say the sound (n).

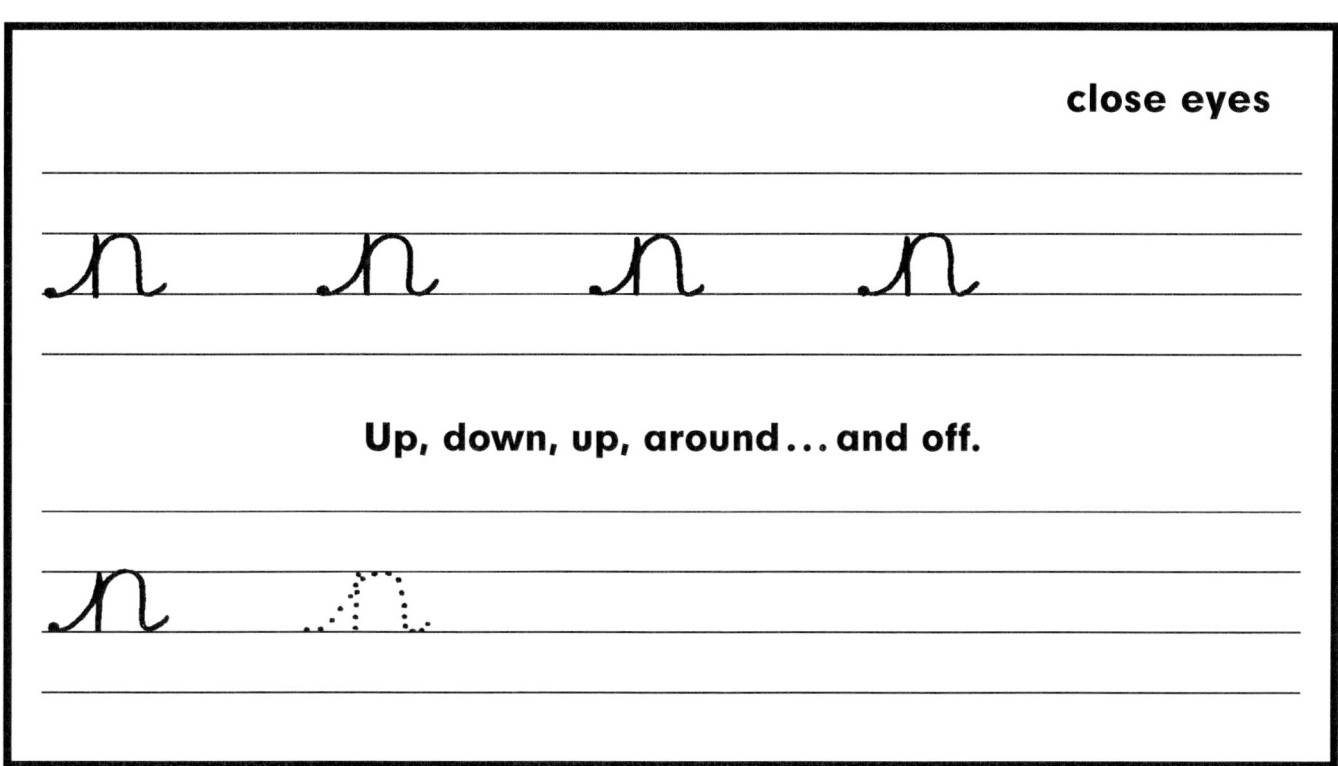

Up, down, up, around... and off.

Trace and say the sound (p).

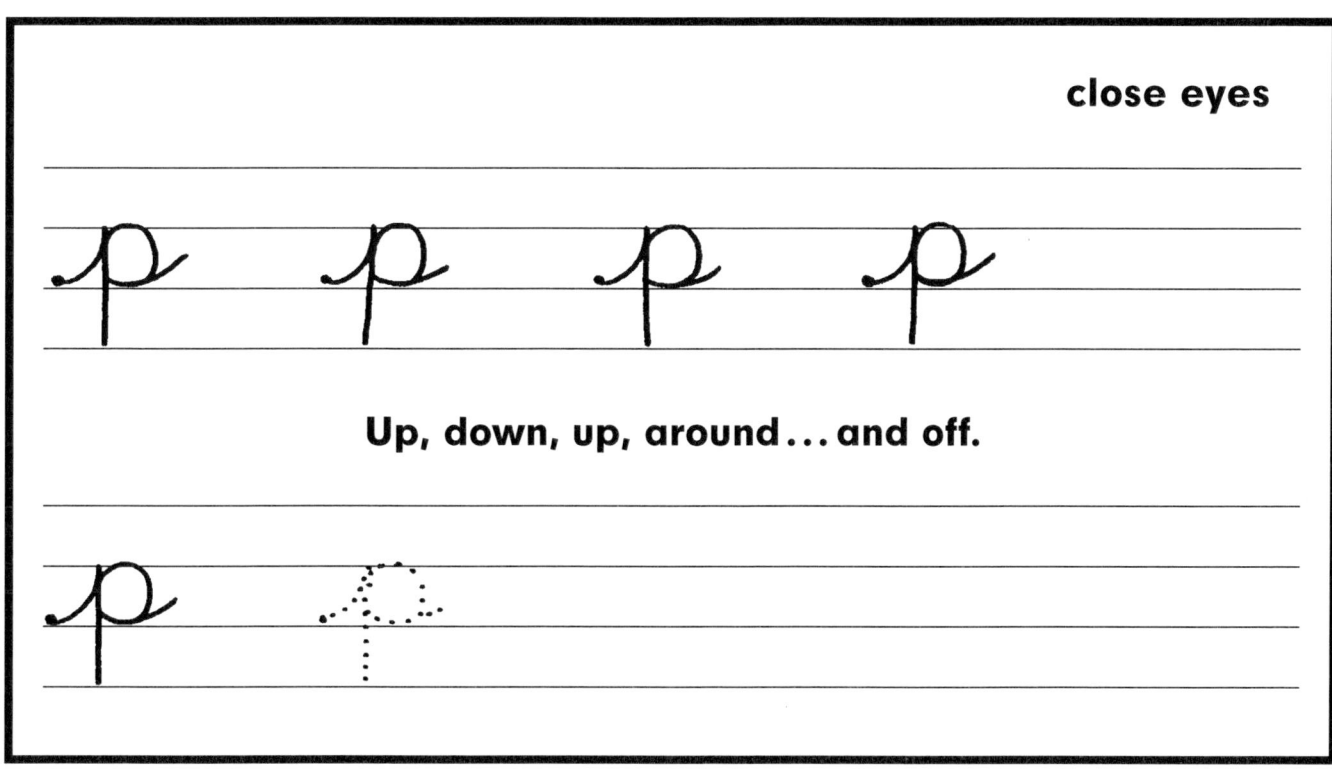

Up, down, up, around... and off.

Lesson 6

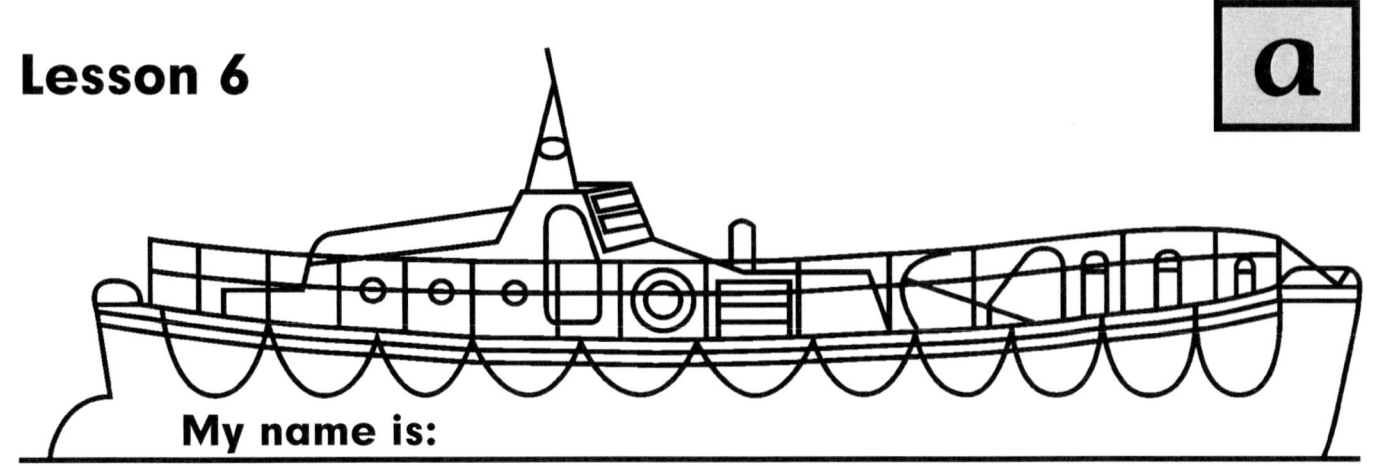

My name is:

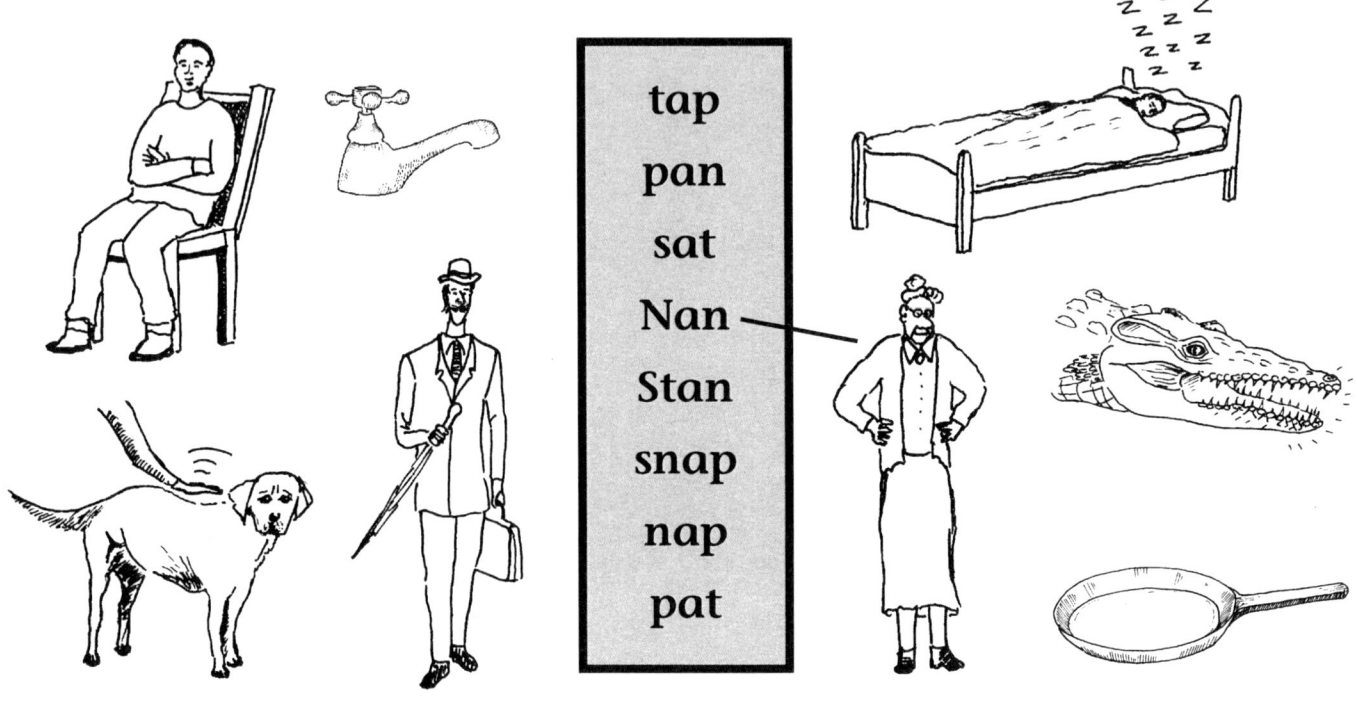

tap
pan
sat
Nan
Stan
snap
nap
pat

Track: a.

```
b e ⓐ d f t u a f b y e a j o p a c g e
b j l a x z a d g b r h f r a v f g h a
x d c y r p o a f q a v j y t l n d c x
a d v c x h k k j d a v x s z a f r a z
y h f a k r s a p u t e h h t l m j b g
d a c x t r h y a x s e a e s g u g f d
s j t a u t r a j t w q a b f r a o a t r
v d a i y p a s e a h t u h d a e r f h
```

Word Match

Circle the same word.

1	**tap**	nap	(tap)	sap	pat
2	**tan**	pan	an	sat	tan
3	**pat**	pat	sat	spat	at
4	**nap**	snap	tap	nap	pan
5	**pan**	nap	tan	Stan	pan
6	**sat**	pat	spat	sat	snap
7	**Stan**	Stan	pan	tan	span
8	**snap**	sap	snap	nap	spat

Spell and Write

Circle the letters. Write the word.

#				
1	(St) sp i (a) (n) t			_Stan_
2	sp sn a i t p			
3	t n a i p t			
4	sn sp a i n p			
5	t p i a s p			
6	i p s a n t			
7	p n a i p n			
8	s p i a n t			

Book 1 | Lesson 6 | Page 3

Read and Choose

#			
1	◯ Stan snaps at the pit.		✓ The tin spins.
2	◯ Stan sat in the tap.		◯ Stan sat in the pan.
3	◯ Tap the tin.		◯ I tip the pin in the tin.
4	◯ Spin the pan.		◯ Spin the pin.
5	◯ I sit in the pit.		◯ It sits in the tin.
6	◯ The pin is in the pan.		◯ I pat the pans.
7	◯ Nan sips it.		◯ It snaps.

Dictation or Look – Say – Cover – Write – Check

1. Stan sat in the pan.

2. It spins in the tin.

3. I pat the pans.

4. Stan snips at it.

5. Tip the pin in the tin.

Handwriting – copy neatly.

a

pat

asp

sat

Listening Skills

Circle the odd one out. Underline the same.

1	<u>pan</u>	(pat)	<u>Nan</u>
2	spat	snap	sap
3	sip	tip	at
4	tin	pit	sit
5	Stan	tip	tan
6	pins	spins	naps
7	spat	sat	sap
8	snip	tin	pin
9	tips	snips	Stan
10	taps	sat	naps

Book 1 | Lesson 6 | Page 6

Cloze Procedure

1 Stan sat in the _____.

2 Is _____ in the pit?

3 The _____ spins.

4 Nan _____ the tip.

5 Stan _____ Nan.

6 I _____ the pins in the pan.

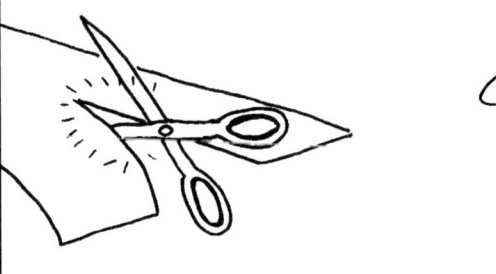
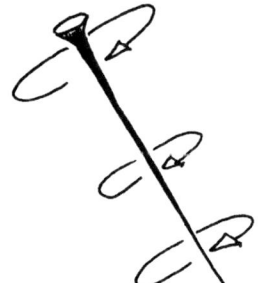

Use these words to complete the sentences.

pin	tip	pan
Nan	taps	snips

Book 1 | Lesson 6 | Page 7

Wordsearch

s	n	i	p	z	s	t	a	d	n
n	s	i	p	i	p	i	g	p	y
a	p	i	t	n	a	p	f	g	h
p	i	n	s	i	t	p	t	j	f
p	n	a	a	n	s	a	p	k	t
a	s	p	t	a	n	t	r	l	i
s	p	i	t	p	i	t	a	q	n
i	n	p	t	a	p	p	y	s	b
S	t	a	n	n	s	a	b	g	d
a	i	t	p	N	a	n	k	h	m
k	f	h	l	r	e	a	d	v	x

Find these words.

pat	pan	sat	nap	tip	tin
nip	spat	snap	tap	tan	Nan
pit	pins	sip	sit	Stan	spit

Lesson 7

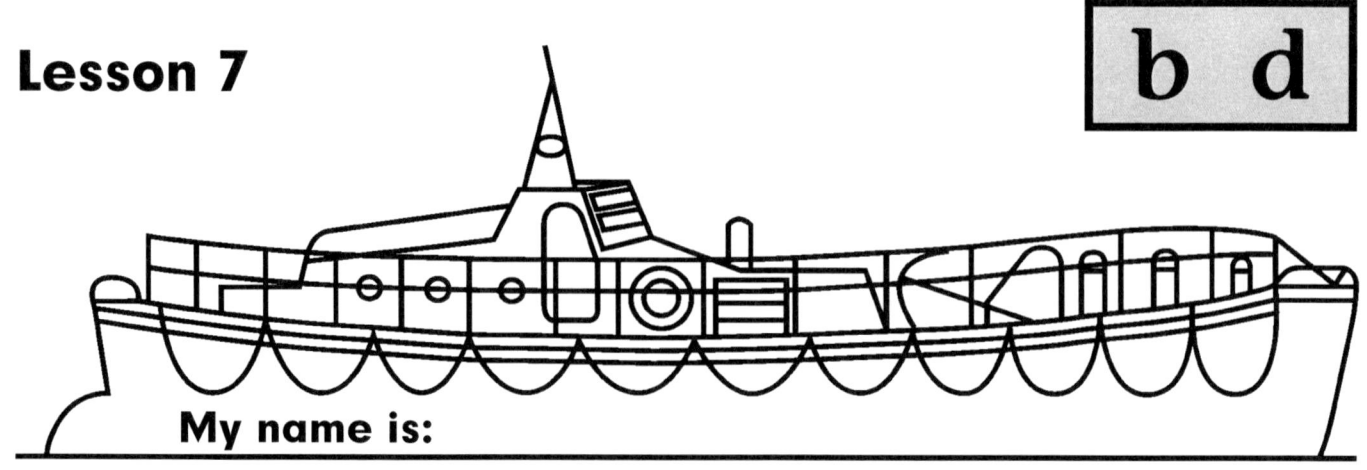

My name is:

b d

Track: **b, d.**

c	d	a	f	e	r	n	b	v	d	i	s	a	g	b	n
c	j	k	l	o	d	s	g	d	u	f	m	q	b	a	r
f	s	c	x	g	b	w	q	r	d	e	i	f	c	x	z
b	d	o	j	m	k	h	d	e	w	u	t	h	l	b	n
f	k	b	a	p	o	r	m	n	k	r	e	w	s	c	i
b	m	o	m	t	u	p	a	v	b	n	q	y	t	r	
e	d	k	l	v	b	i	r	t	s	m	z	k	n	m	l
b	p	t	h	d	s	c	v	n	w	u	k	l	d	m	b
c	a	x	b	e	w	g	v	g	t	v	d	c	n	h	k
l	p	y	x	o	b	k	q	b	f	e	i	g	b	h	d
b	u	y	g	b	w	s	d	c	z	g	h	d	k	b	

Circle the same letter.

b	ⓑ	t	f	r	ⓑ
d	m	d	g	d	b
b	h	b	d	b	b
d	t	i	f	d	d
d	p	d	d	b	k
b	i	b	d	b	b
b	t	d	b	n	b
d	d	p	d	b	d

Draw a line from the b to the pictures with a (b) sound in them.

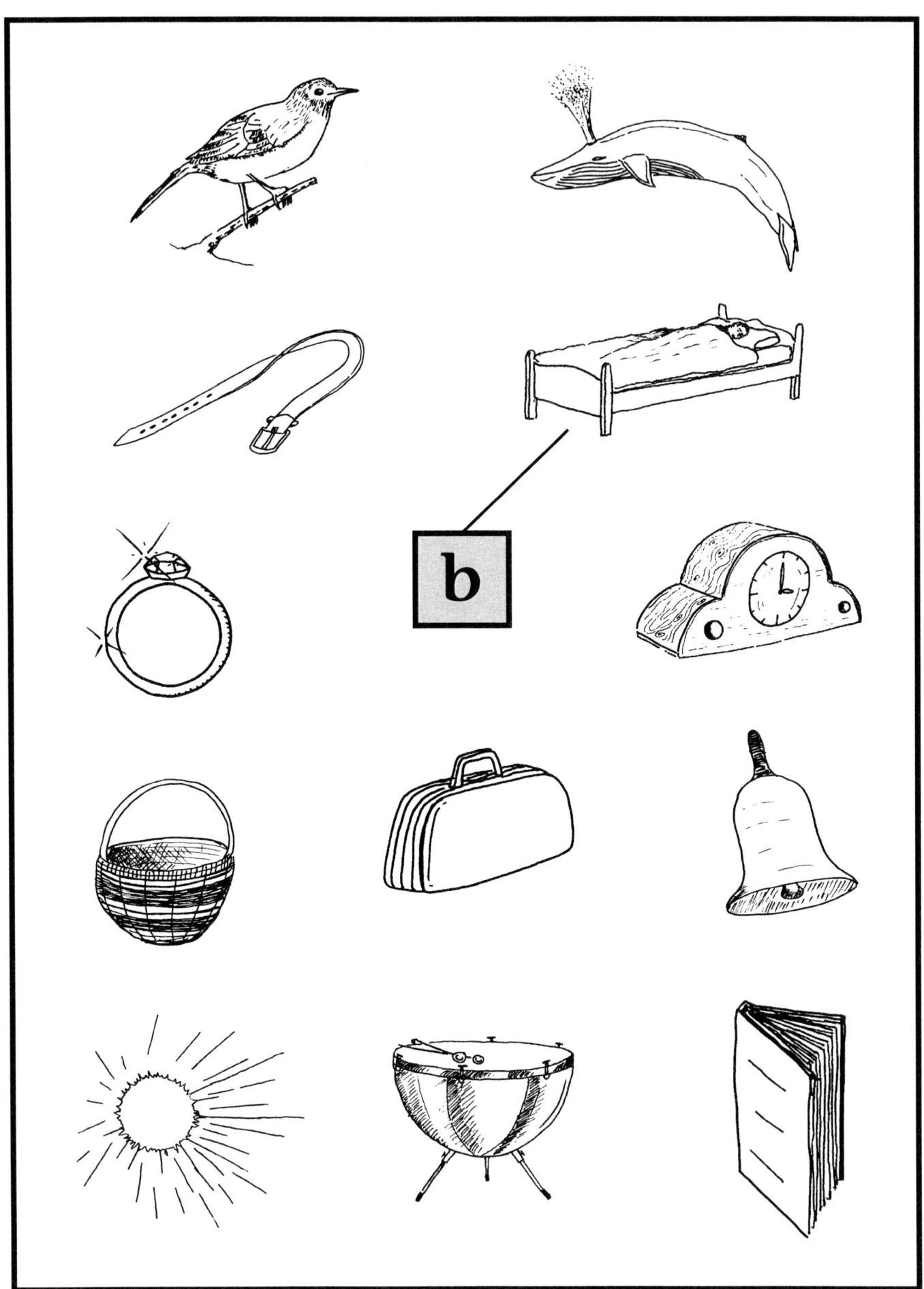

Draw a line from the d to the pictures with a (d) sound in them.

Say the name of each picture.
Print the beginning or end b, d sound you hear.

Joined Handwriting

Trace and say the sound (b).

close eyes

Up, down, up, around... and off.

Trace and say the sound (d).

close eyes

Up, stop... back, around, up, down... and off.

Joined Handwriting

Copy neatly.

Remember... the **looks like this:** *the*

1   Dan did tip it in the bin.

_____

2   Sid dips the tip in a pan.

_____

3   Dad did sit in the pit.

_____

4   Pat taps the bad bat.

_____

Wordsearch

b	s	D	p	a	b	i	t
a	b	a	t	s	t	p	t
d	i	n	n	S	i	d	d
a	n	f	i	s	a	d	a
b	a	n	b	e	d	i	d
p	a	d	i	d	t	p	s
d	i	d	d	t	a	b	p

Find these words.

bin	din	bat	bad
Sid	ban	did	nib
dip	Dan	tab	sad
pad	bid	bit	dad

Book 1 | Lesson 7 | Page 8

Lesson 8

sn sp st

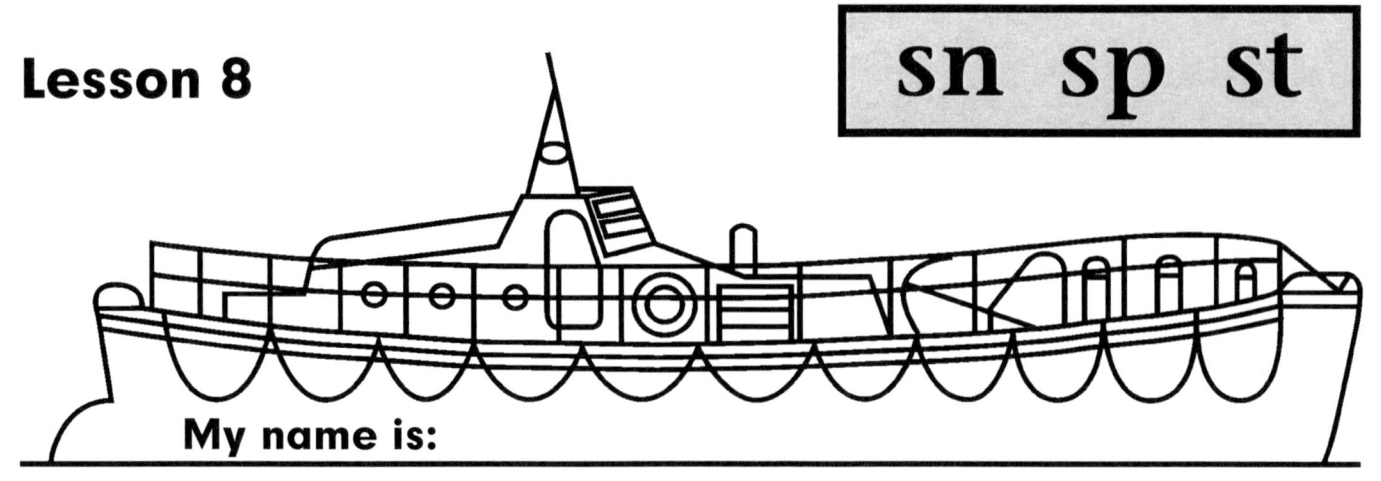

My name is:

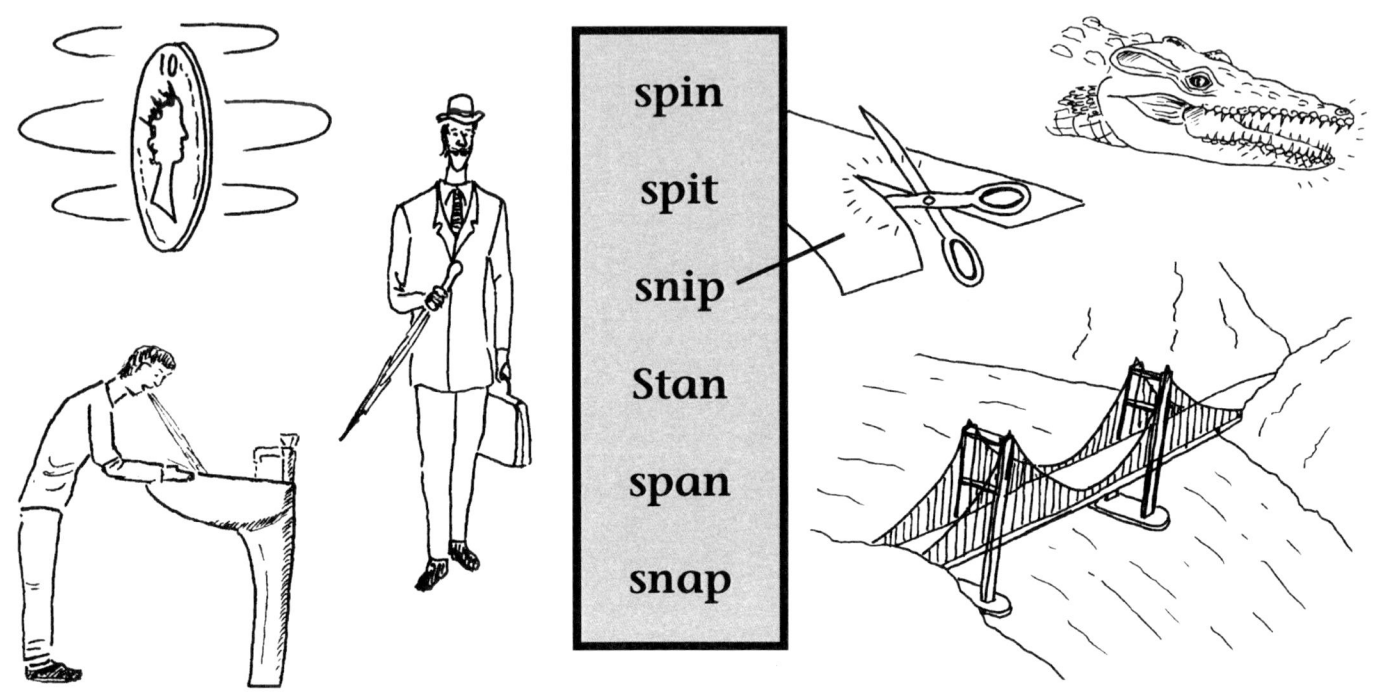

Track: **sn, sp, st.**

bid	Stan	spin	bad	spit
sad	span	pad	did	bin
bit	snip	dad	snap	tab
snip	Sid	bat	spat	tip
pit	spins	snaps	nap	snips
sit	pins	tins	spits	pats
stab	stabs	spin	sat	bit

Word Match

Circle the same word.

1	**Stan**	tan	sit	(Stan)	snap
2	**spin**	pin	spin	spit	snip
3	**span**	sin	pan	spat	span
4	**spit**	spit	spin	span	pit
5	**snip**	sip	nip	snip	snap
6	**stab**	Stan	stab	stabs	tab
7	**snap**	sap	nap	snip	snap
8	**asp**	snap	as	asp	span

Spell and Write

Circle the letters. Write the word.

1	n i t	a s p		asp
2	sp a n	s i s		
3	sn i p	sp s t		
4	st p n	sp a t		
5	st i p	sn a s		
6	sp a n	St t p		
7	p i t	b a d	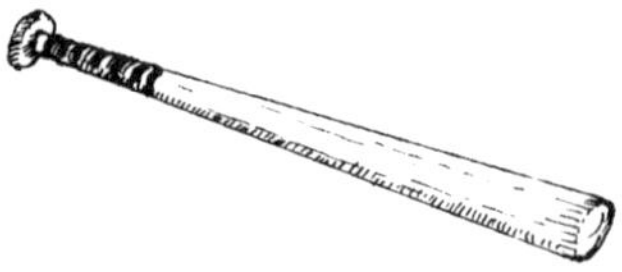	
8	d a p	t s b	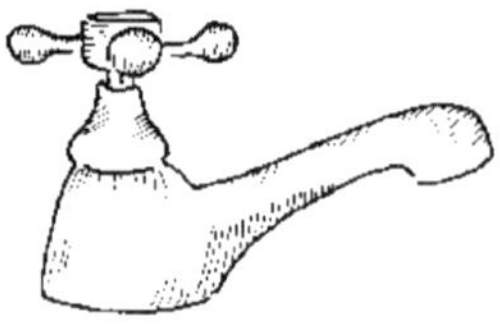	

Read and Choose

1	◯ Stan bit the tin.		✓ The tin is a bit sad!
2	◯ Spin the pin.		◯ The pin is in the tap.
3	◯ Pip snaps the bat.		◯ Did the tab snap?
4	◯ Sid pats the tap.		◯ The tap is in the bin.
5	◯ I stab the pad.		◯ I tap the pad.
6	◯ The asp sits in the pan.		◯ Did the asp spit?
7	◯ The asp nips Nan.		◯ Nan naps and tans.

Dictation or Look – Say – Cover – Write – Check

1   Stan snips his pad.

   _____

2   Is a tap in the pit?

   _____

3   Tip the pin in the tin.

   _____

4   Sid spits at the sap.

   _____

Handwriting – copy neatly.

sp

st

sn

asp

Listening Skills

Circle the odd one out. Underline the same.

#			
1	<u>snap</u>	(tip)	<u>nap</u>
2	tip	snip	nap
3	pad	span	tan
4	spit	bid	sit
5	tab	stab	span
6	bid	Sid	pan
7	stab	dad	bad
8	bin	span	tin
9	tap	snip	sap
10	pan	Stan	snap

Book 1 | Lesson 8 | Page 6

Cloze Procedure

1 _____ bit the tin.

2 _____ the pin.

3 Pat the _____ spits _____ the tap.

4 Sad dad _____ the _____.

5 Nan sits _____ the pit.

6 I _____ the bat.

Use these words to complete the sentences.

asp	snap	Stan	tips
in	Spin	at	bin

Wordsearch

S	d	s	f	t	h	u	k	l	e
q	t	p	d	g	a	t	j	m	i
s	n	a	p	s	e	f	y	h	s
a	c	n	n	s	r	s	h	a	v
a	w	e	r	s	p	i	n	d	n
x	S	u	b	f	t	i	g	i	l
d	i	j	i	g	a	a	t	n	p
s	d	i	d	h	p	s	b	h	k
c	b	n	b	h	k	y	u	i	r
i	n	s	m	a	r	t	i	a	h
f	h	e	y	i	t	f	e	g	s

Find these words.

Stan	spin	spit	span	snip	snap
stab	Sid	bat	bid	did	tap
it	in	is	at	as	an

Book 1 | Lesson 8 | Page 8

Lesson 9

-nd -nt

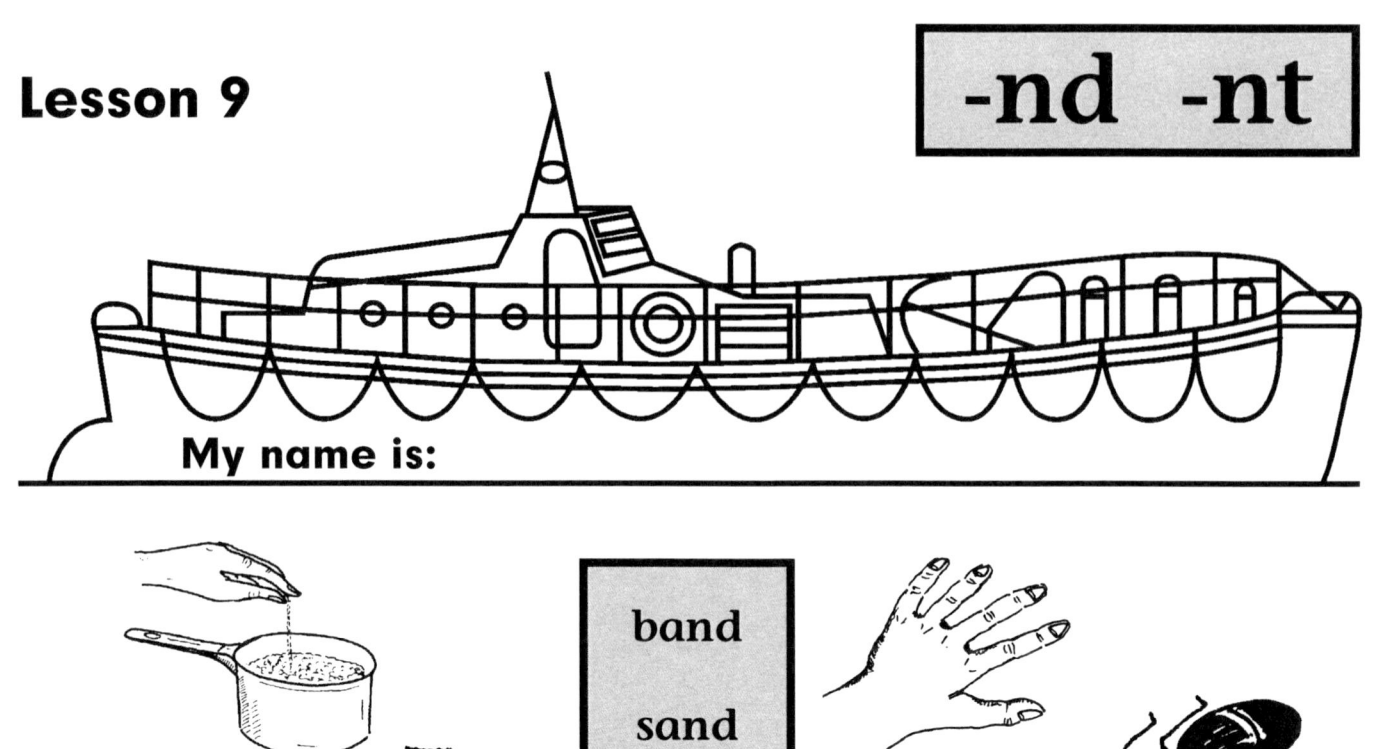

My name is:

band
sand
hand
ant
tint
hint

Track: **nd, nt.**

band	tin	ant	sin	pant
dip	sand	in	hand	it
stand	stab	pin	bin	and
pant	snip	tint	hip	is
dip	dint	pit	hand	it
and	sip	band	ant	dip
hint	dip	dint	stab	tint
snip	tip	ant	hand	sip

Word Match

Circle the same word.

#					
1	**and**	an	ant	(and)	hand
2	**band**	hand	and	dint	band
3	**ant**	an	ant	and	sand
4	**dint**	dint	tint	in	tin
5	**pant**	ant	pant	sand	an
6	**hand**	and	ant	band	hand
7	**tint**	tint	in	tin	dint
8	**sand**	an	and	sand	hand

Book 1 | Lesson 9 | Page 2

Spell and Write

Circle the letters. Write the word.

#	Letters	Picture	Word
1	(a) o / (nt) i	ant	_ant_
2	b d / a i / nd nt	headband	_____
3	h d / i a / nt nd	hand	_____
4	t s / i a / nt nd	sand	_____
5	a o / nt nd	me — you (and)	_____
6	d b / i a / nt nd	car (band)	_____
7	sn st / a i / b nd	sit	_____
8	sn st / i a / p d	snap	_____

Book 1 | Lesson 9 | Page 3

Read and Choose

#			
1	☑ Pip is in the sandpit.		○ Sam has sand in his hand.
2	○ The band is in his hand.		○ Stan has a band.
3	○ The ant is on the pin.		○ The pin in the bin has an ant on it.
4	○ Nan has a hint.		○ The ant tans.
5	○ The tin has a dint in it.		○ The pin has a dint in it.
6	○ Dan pants in the sandpit.		○ Dan nips Nan.
7	○ Sand is in the tip.		○ Sand is in the pit.

Book 1 Lesson 9 Page 4

Dictation or Look – Say – Cover – Write – Check

1 The asp is in his hand.

2 Stan the ant is in the tap.

3 Sid and Tip dip in the pin tin.

4 The tin has a dint in it.

5 Snip the pad.

Handwriting – copy neatly.

nt

nd

end

stand

Listening Skills

Circle the odd one out. Underline the same.

1	<u>and</u>	<u>hand</u>	(pant)
2	pant	stand	ant
3	band	sand	it
4	dint	in	hint
5	it	pant	ant
6	sand	stab	and
7	sad	bad	spin
8	pad	tip	sip
9	stand	and	at
10	sand	tap	snap

Cloze Procedure

1 Dan the _____ is in the tin.

2 The tin had a _____ in it.

3 The _____ is in the _____ pit.

4 Stan _____ Pip
sit in the _____.

5 Dan has sand in his _____.

6 The _____ has
a pin in it.

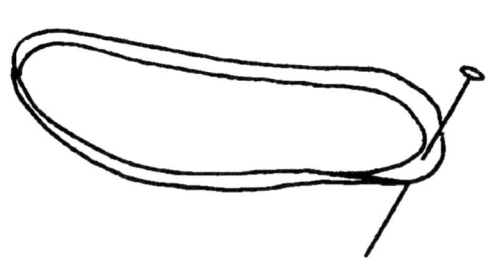

Use these words to complete the sentences.

| ant | hand | pin | band |
| asp | and | bin | sand |

Wordsearch

p	f	e	g	n	j	l	s	a	f
e	a	f	h	s	e	i	u	p	l
a	d	n	h	k	i	p	a	n	t
w	r	t	a	n	d	b	n	l	i
a	e	r	n	g	i	d	t	k	n
s	a	n	d	k	n	d	t	e	t
s	a	c	b	i	t	n	i	s	g
d	t	h	k	l	o	s	d	r	p
s	x	a	b	a	n	d	p	t	h
s	e	t	n	m	l	i	p	i	f
a	w	e	r	d	b	n	h	i	n

Find these words.

and	hand	sand	pant	ant	tint
dint	band	spin	pan	stand	is

Lesson 10

Review and Post-test

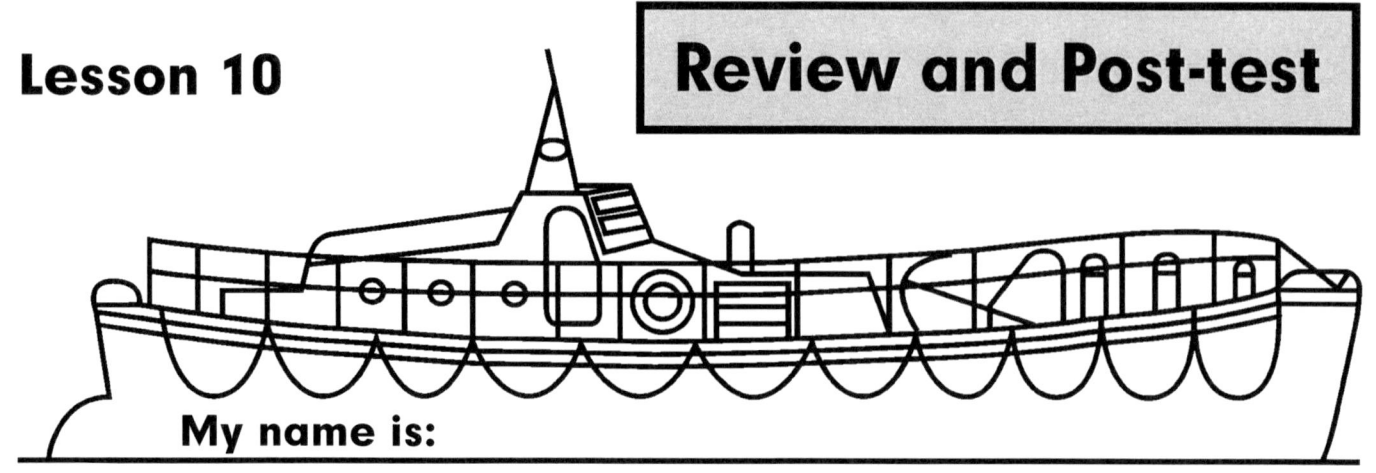

My name is:

Track: Words with a.

it	at	nap	pan	nip
Dan	is	sip	Nan	tin
pins	in	tan	nap	Stan
sit	hand	snap	pat	sin
stand	sat	pit	sap	tip
snap	tap	hat	hit	as
spit	an	his	snip	span

Word Match

Circle the same word.

1	**snap**	sap	nap	snip	(snap)
2	**pan**	pat	pan	pin	pad
3	**spin**	pin	spit	spin	pins
4	**bad**	dad	sad	had	bad
5	**hand**	sand	and	hand	had
6	**snip**	snip	nips	snap	tips
7	**hint**	tint	hint	hit	hid
8	**tin**	tip	tint	tin	pin

Spell and Write

Circle the letters. Write the word.

#	Letters		Picture	Word
1	st, (a), nt	(sp), i, (n)	bridge	_span_
2	h, a, nd	d, i, d	hand	
3	s, i, p	sn, a, nt	snapped pencil	
4	N, i, st	t, a, n	man	
5	p, a, nd	s, i, nt	sand	
6	t, a, s	s, i, n	sun	
7	n, a, nt	b, i, p	bed	
8	Sp, i, n	St, a, nd	man	

Book 1 | Lesson 10 | Page 3

Read and Choose

1	✓ The ants sit in the sandpit.	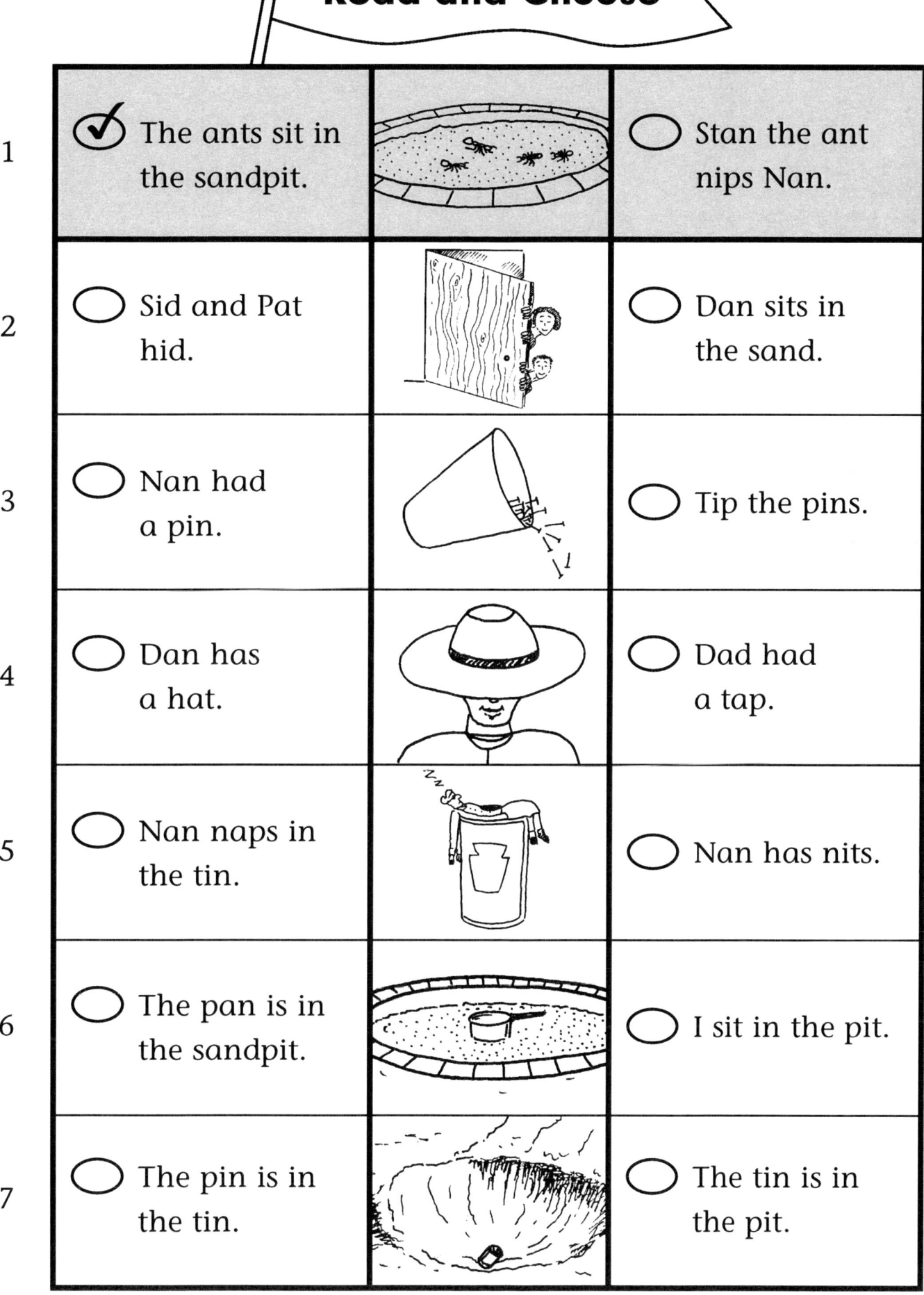	◯ Stan the ant nips Nan.
2	◯ Sid and Pat hid.		◯ Dan sits in the sand.
3	◯ Nan had a pin.		◯ Tip the pins.
4	◯ Dan has a hat.		◯ Dad had a tap.
5	◯ Nan naps in the tin.		◯ Nan has nits.
6	◯ The pan is in the sandpit.		◯ I sit in the pit.
7	◯ The pin is in the tin.		◯ The tin is in the pit.

Dictation or Look – Say – Cover – Write – Check

1. Dan has ants in his pants.

2. The asp sits in the sandpit.

3. Stan the ant hid in the tin.

4. Dad has a band in his hat.

5. Did Stan the ant nip Nan?

Handwriting – copy neatly.

i

st

a

nd

Listening Skills

Circle the odd one out. Underline the same.

#			
1	<u>pin</u>	<u>pit</u>	(pat)
2	sat	pat	sit
3	Pip	Nan	Stan
4	pant	ant	and
5	it	an	is
6	ban	did	Sid
7	as	at	in
8	sit	pit	hid
9	tint	hand	sand
10	nap	spit	tap

Cloze Procedure

1 Dan tips the _____.

2 Is _____ in the pit?

3 Stan had a _____.

4 _____ the pin in the _____.

5 Pip _____ his _____ in the pan.

6 Pat _____ the band in the tap.

Use these words to complete the sentences.

tap	Spin	Nan	hand
pan	hid	sand	dips

Wordsearch

s	n	a	p	g	h	a	e	y	i
a	t	g	h	i	a	s	h	k	l
n	i	a	i	h	n	s	e	r	t
d	n	c	n	u	d	s	w	r	i
a	w	e	t	d	n	i	n	m	p
a	w	r	u	i	l	t	i	i	n
w	a	a	x	c	p	g	t	h	p
i	t	s	b	m	a	d	s	g	u
s	t	v	p	l	n	d	v	s	e
z	n	i	t	s	l	a	e	y	i
a	t	j	u	o	p	r	p	s	h

Find these words.

pins	sit	hand	pan	stand	snap
tip	tin	sand	snip	hint	nap
nits	asp	at	in	it	as

Answers to Lesson 1

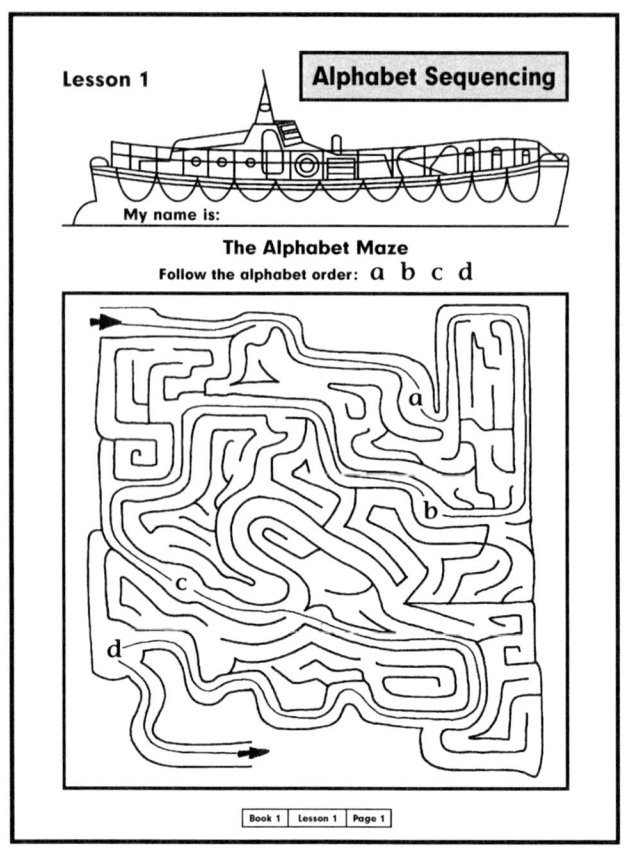
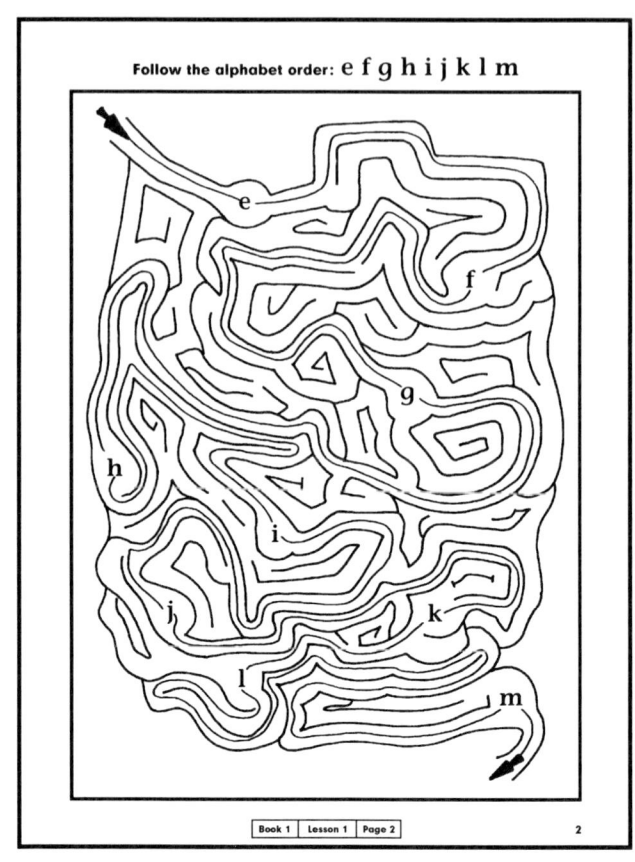

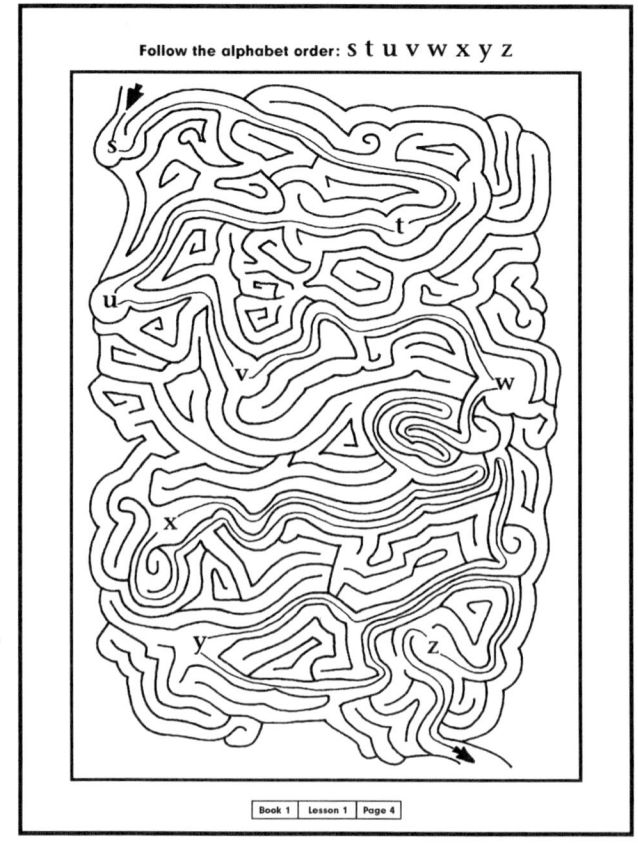

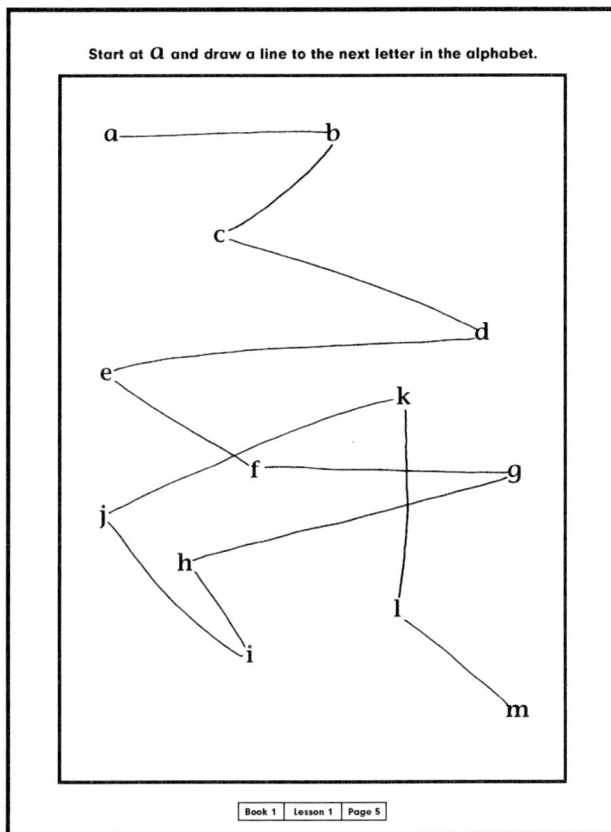

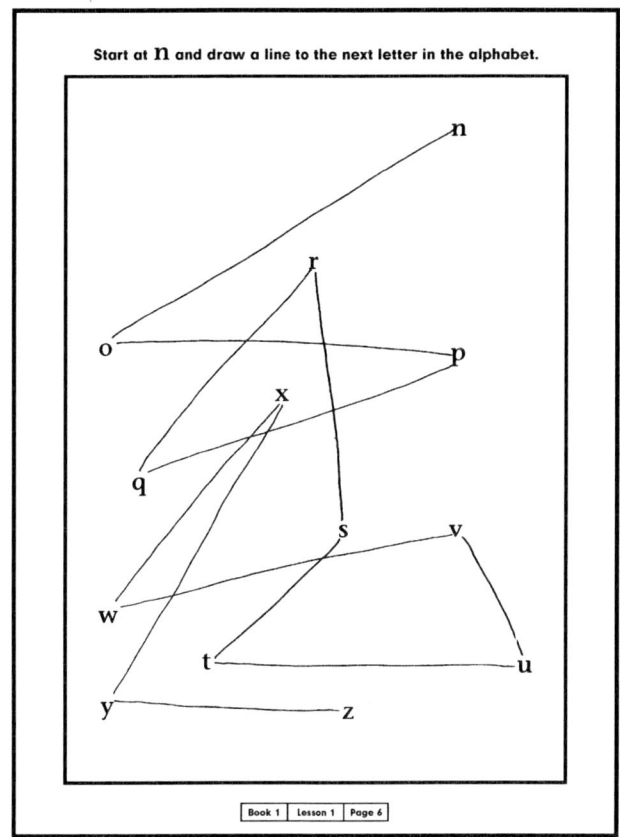

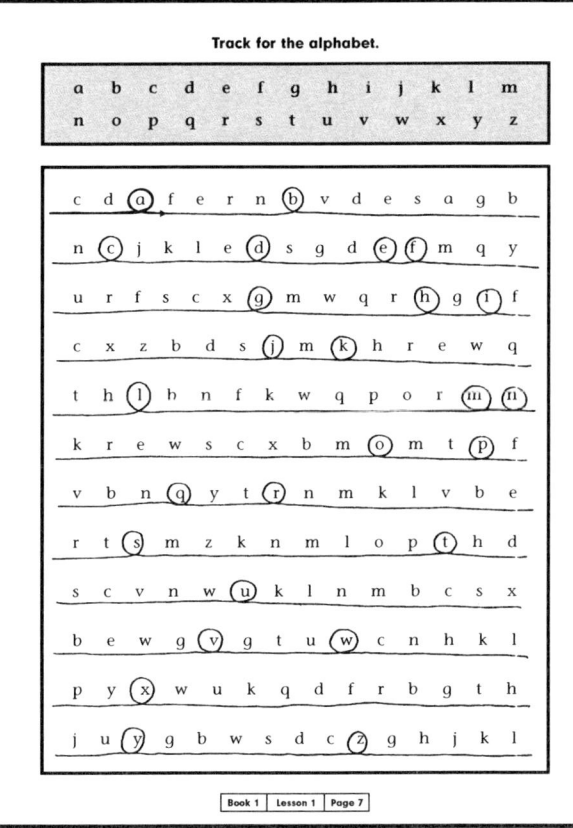

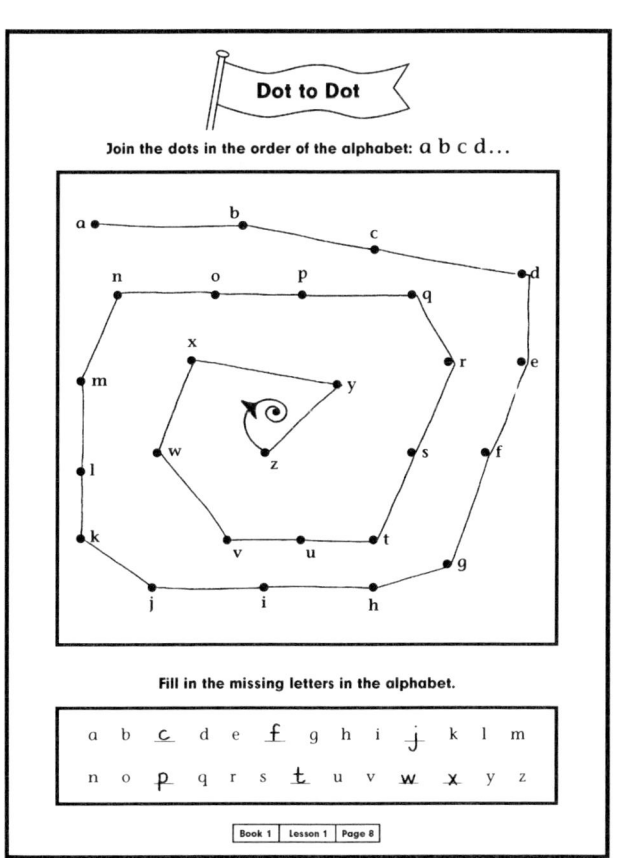

Answers to Lesson 2

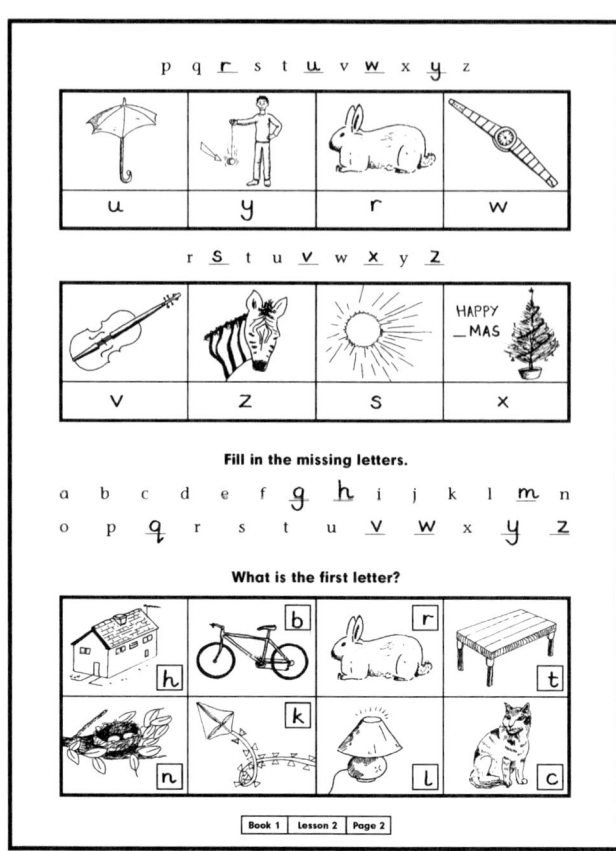
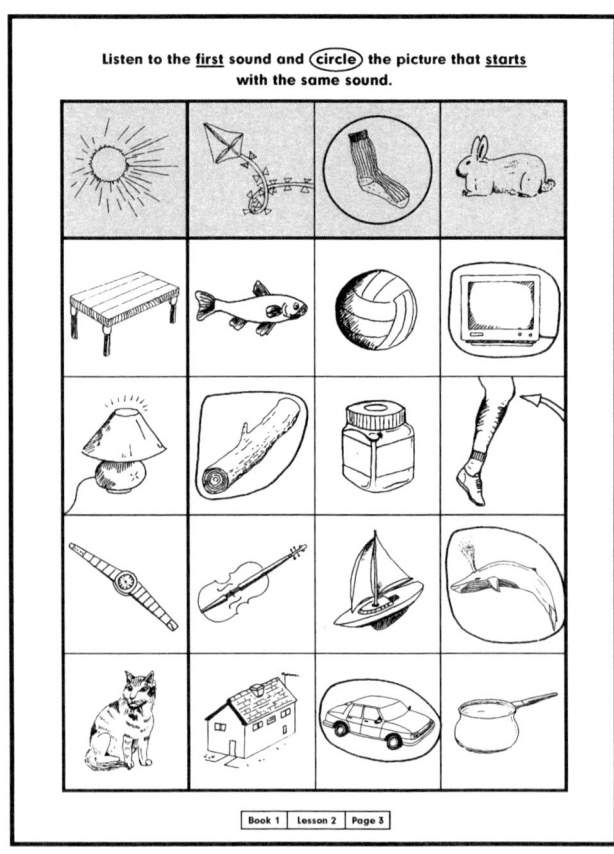
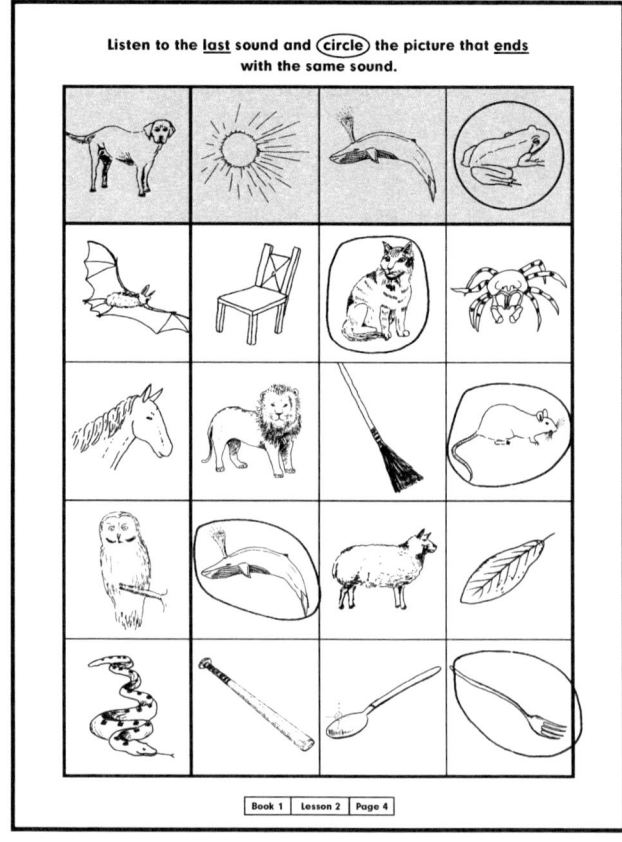

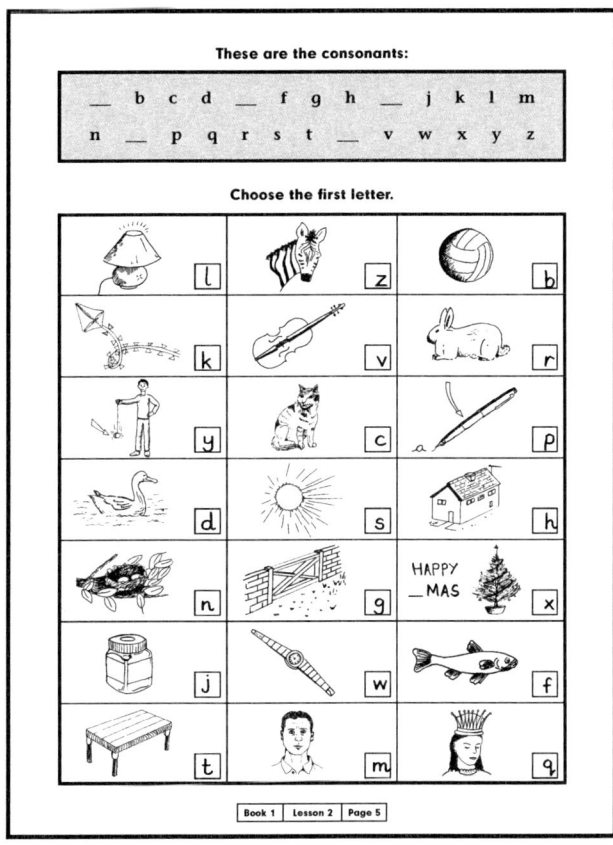
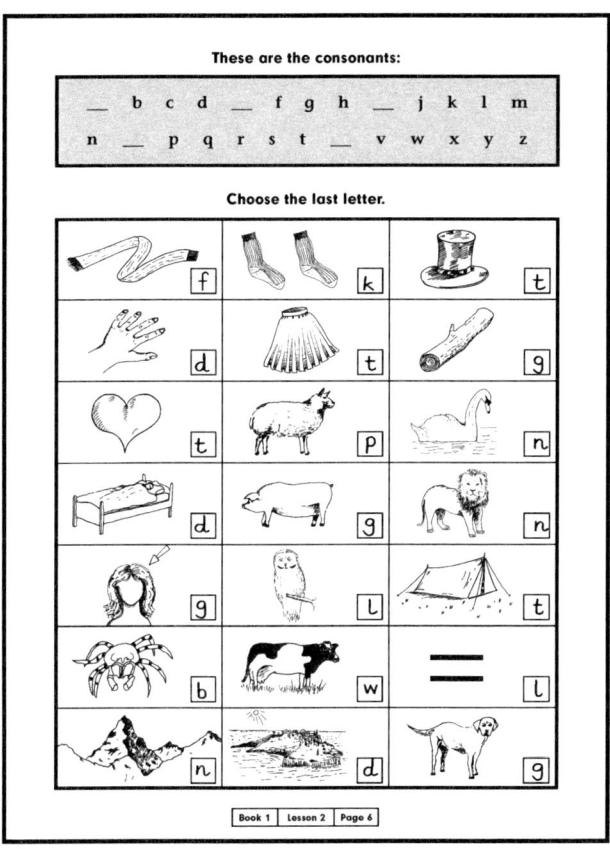

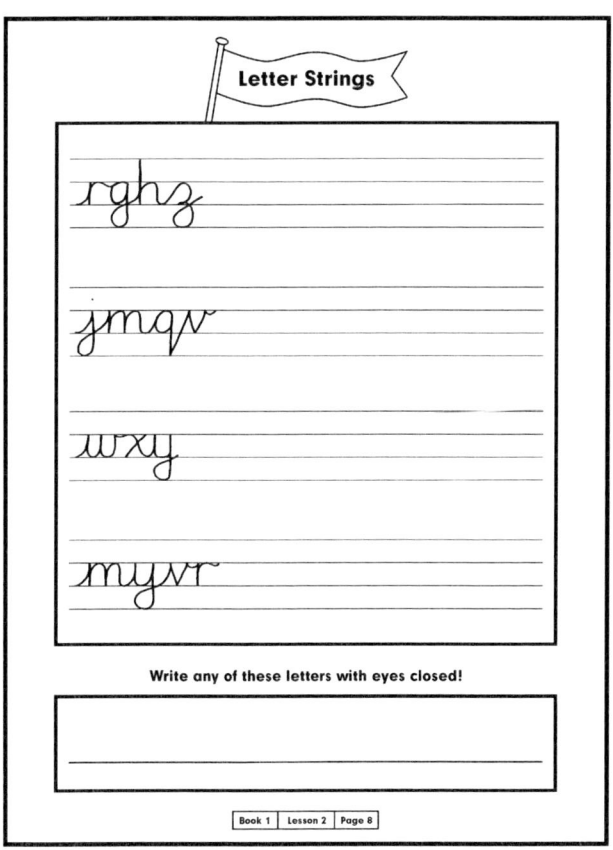

Answers to Lesson 3

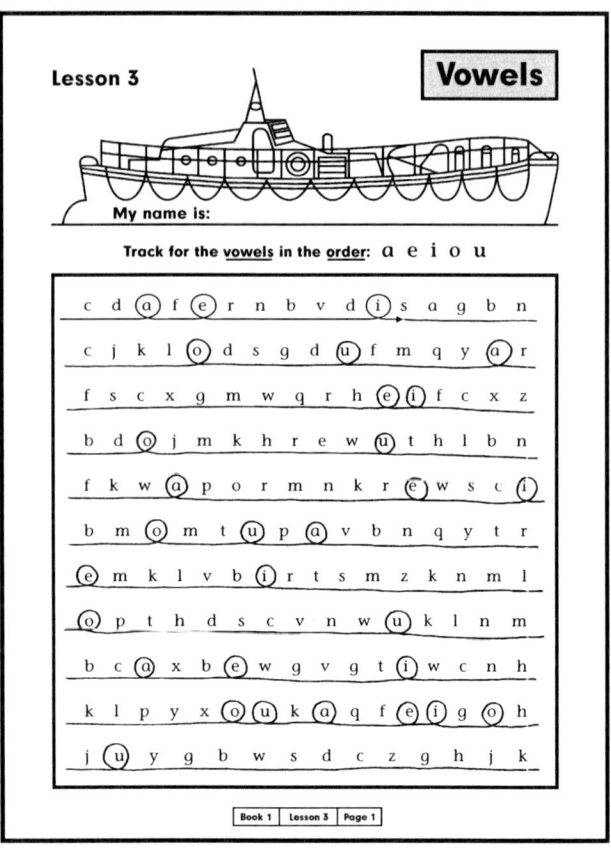
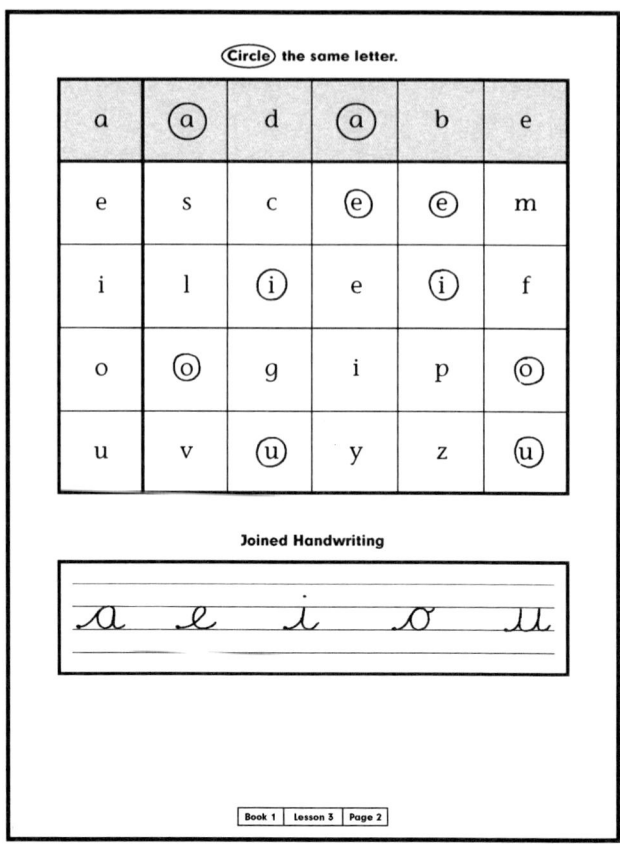
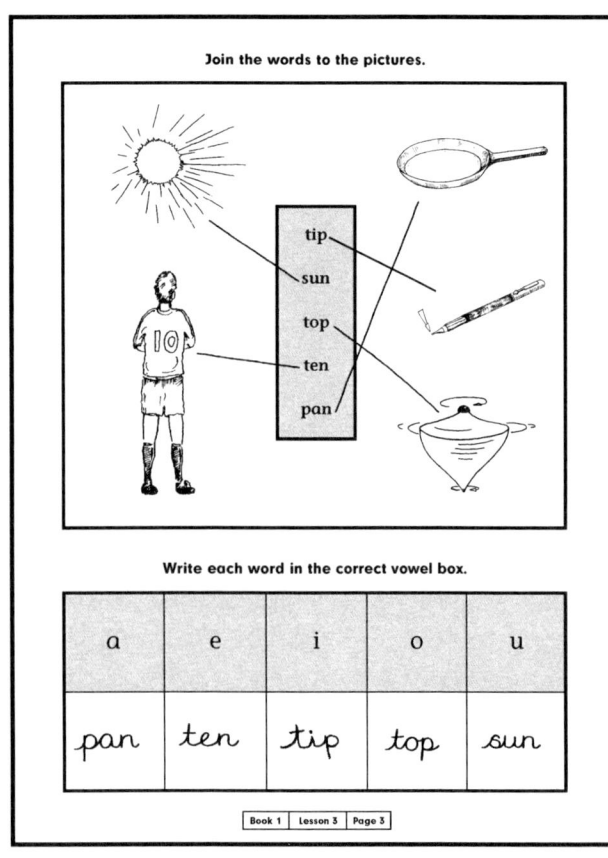
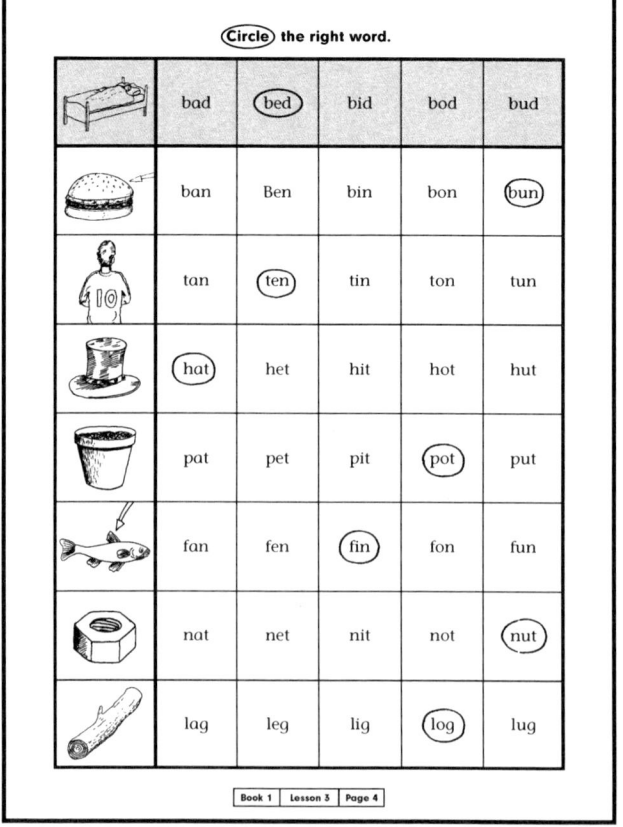

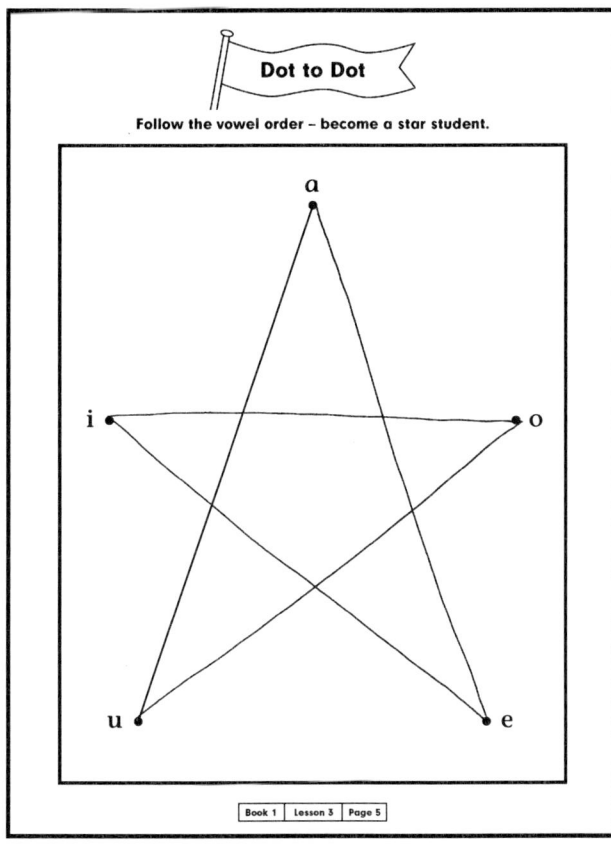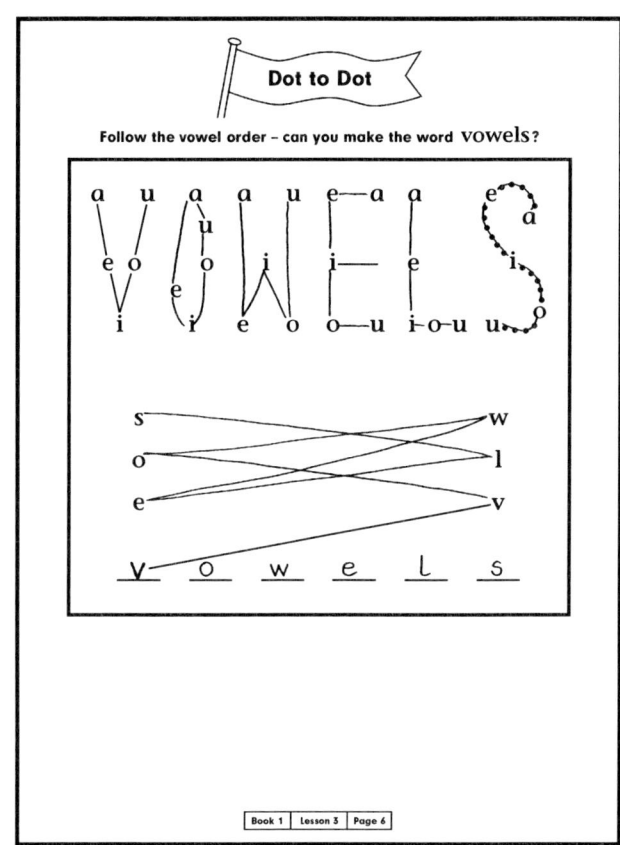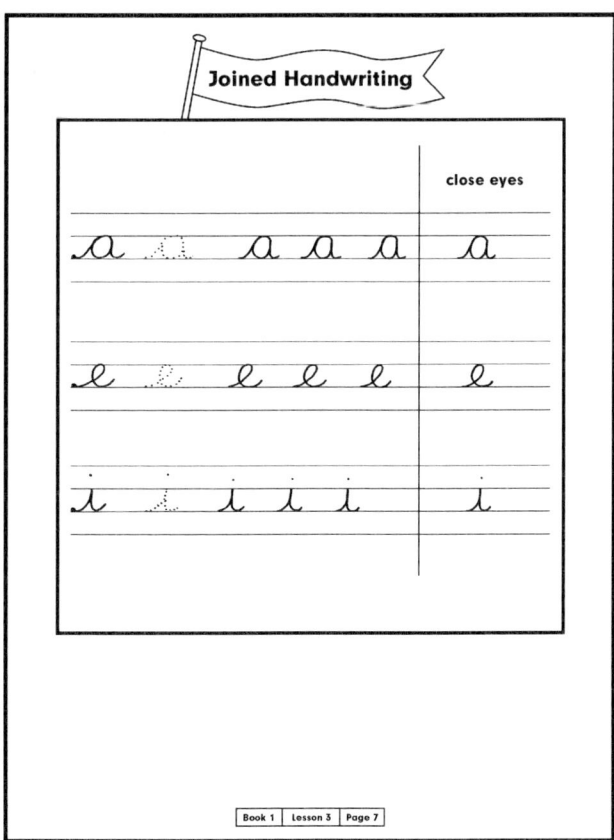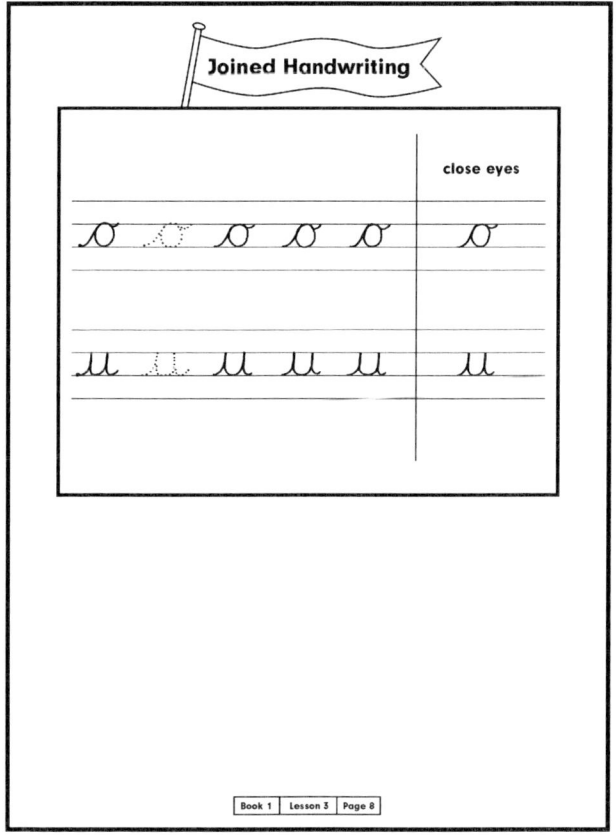

Answers to Lesson 4

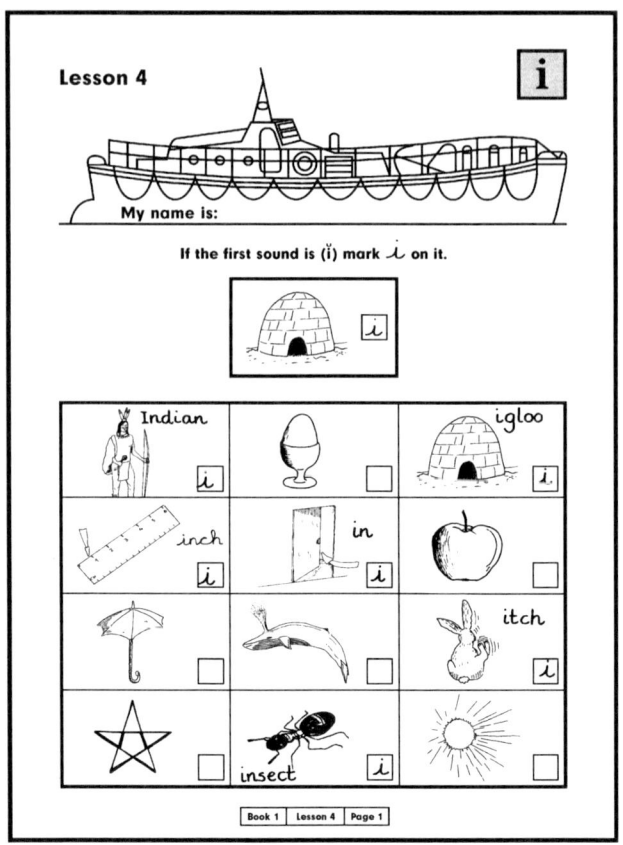
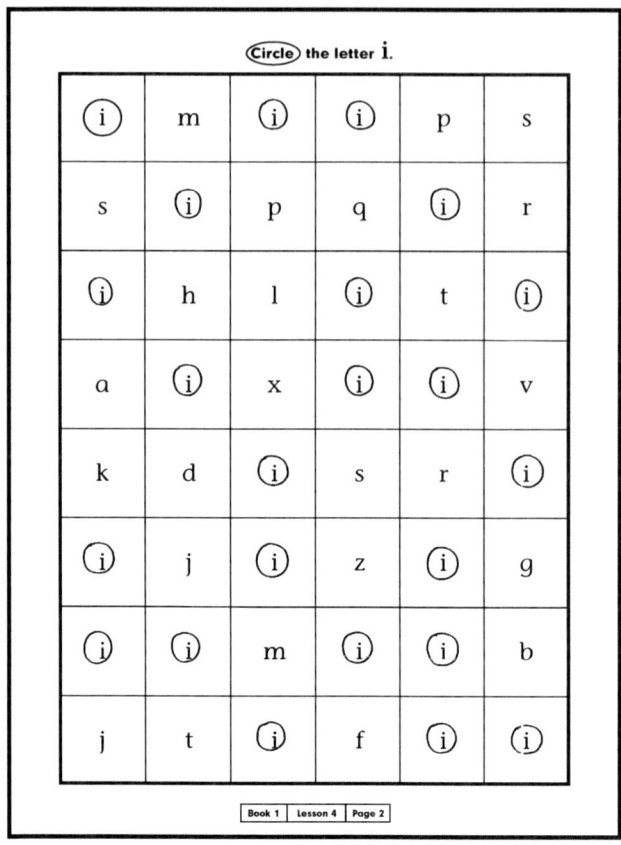
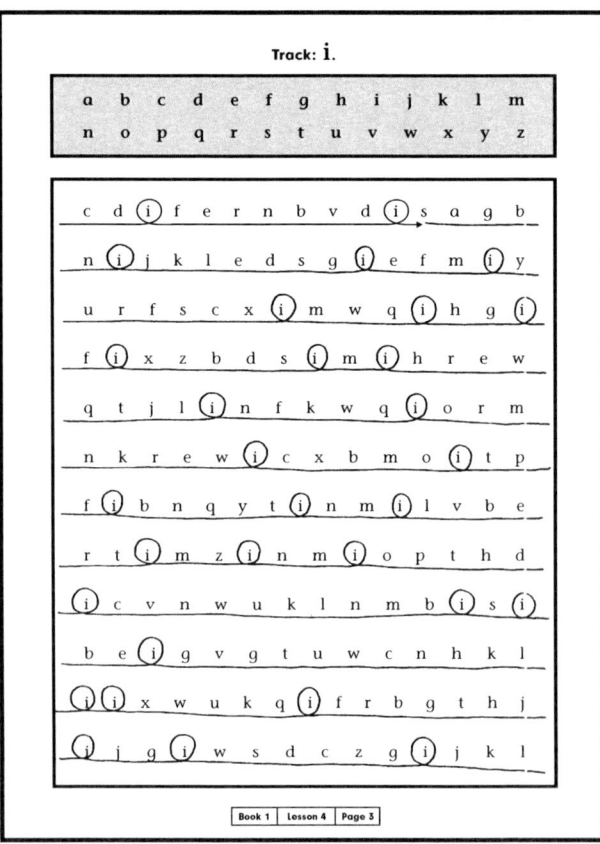
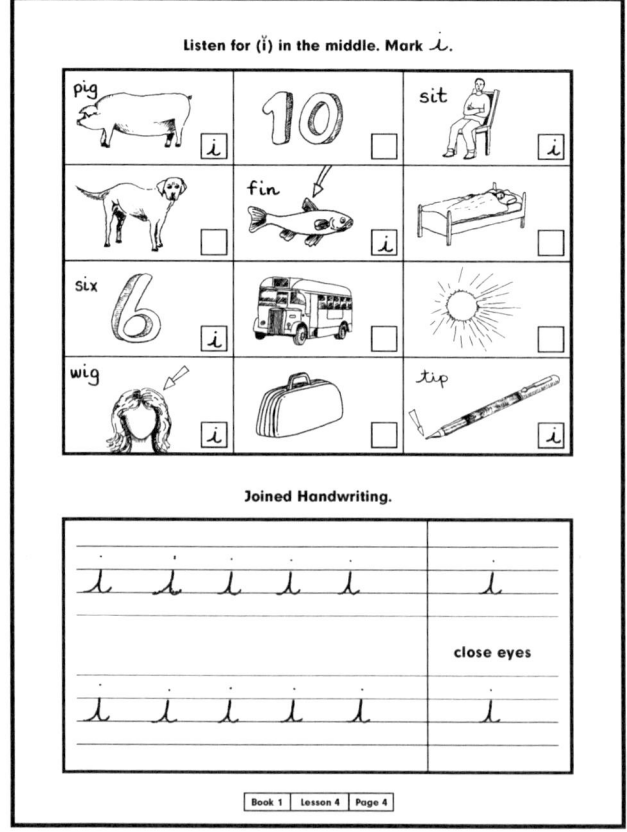

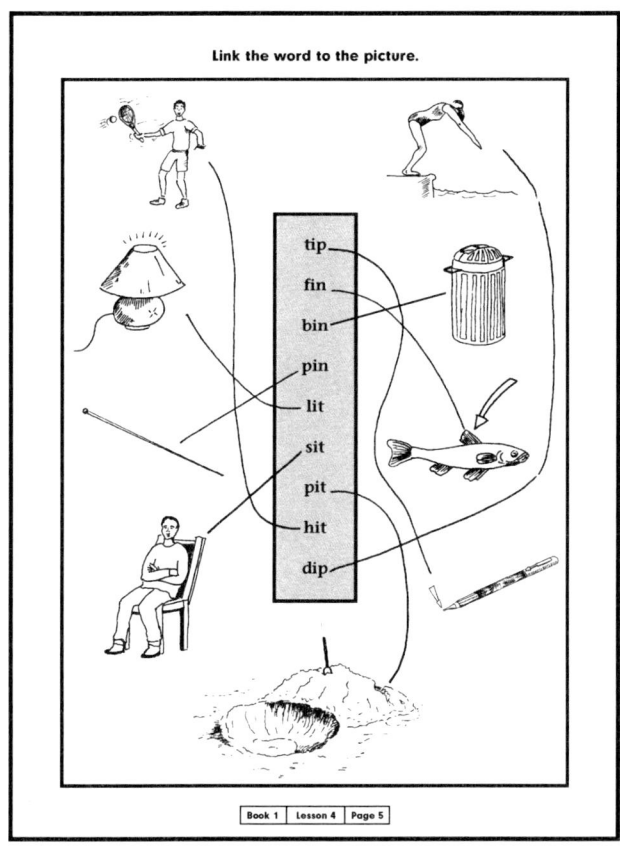
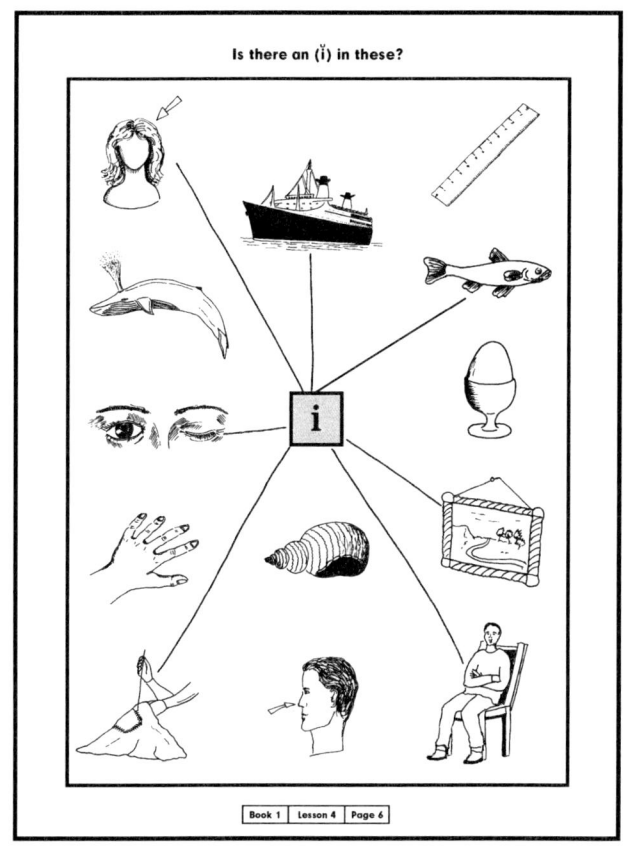
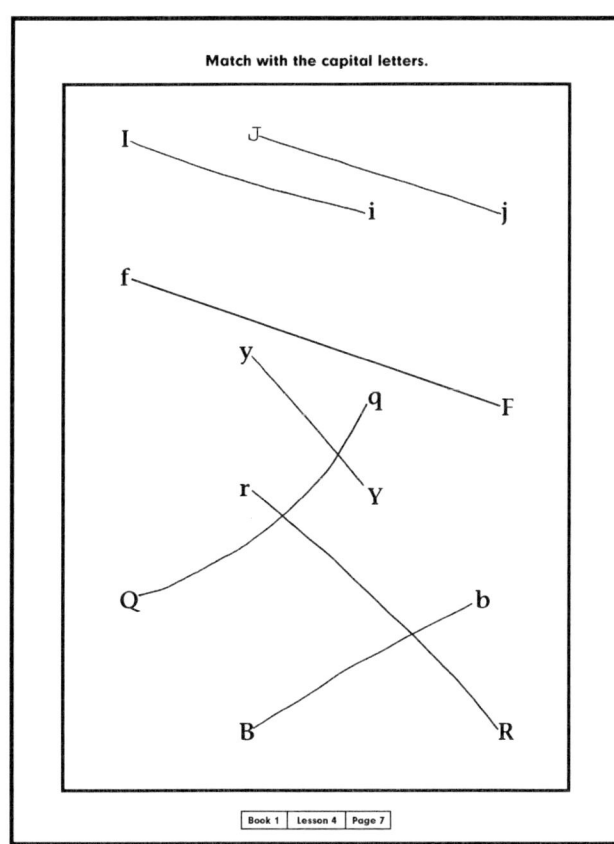
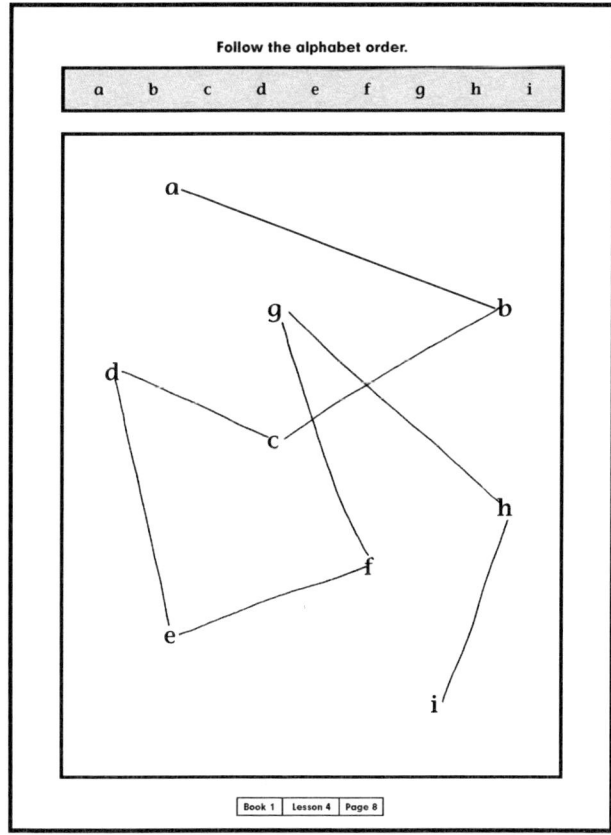

Answers to Lesson 5

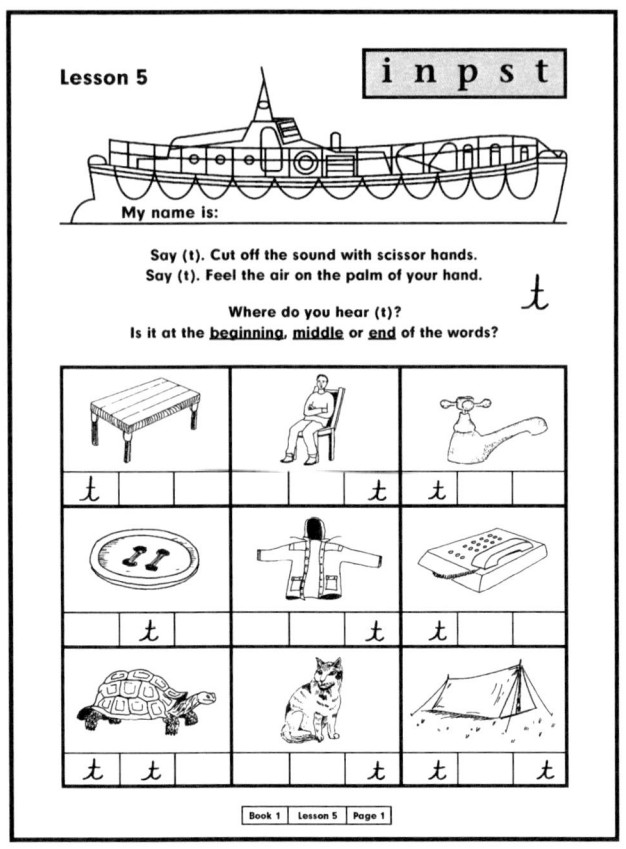
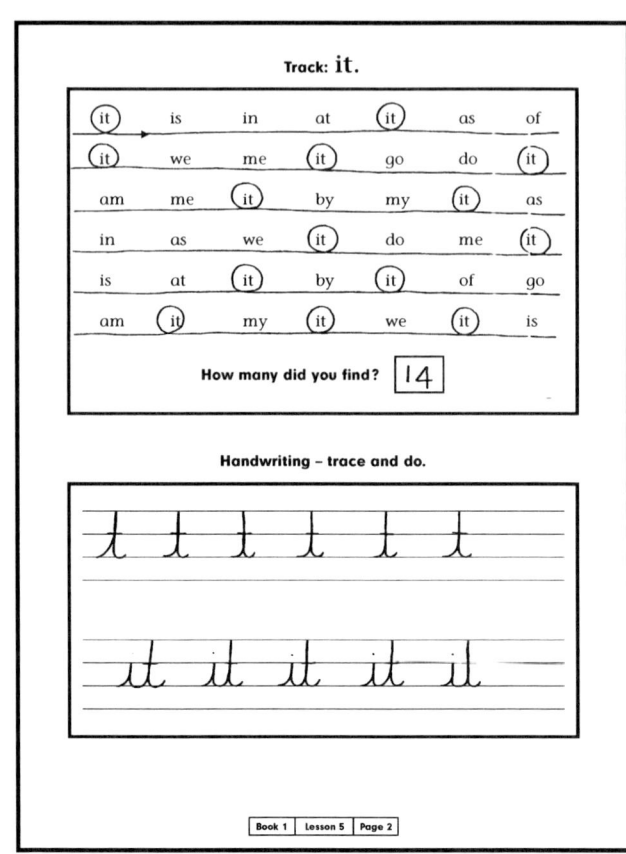
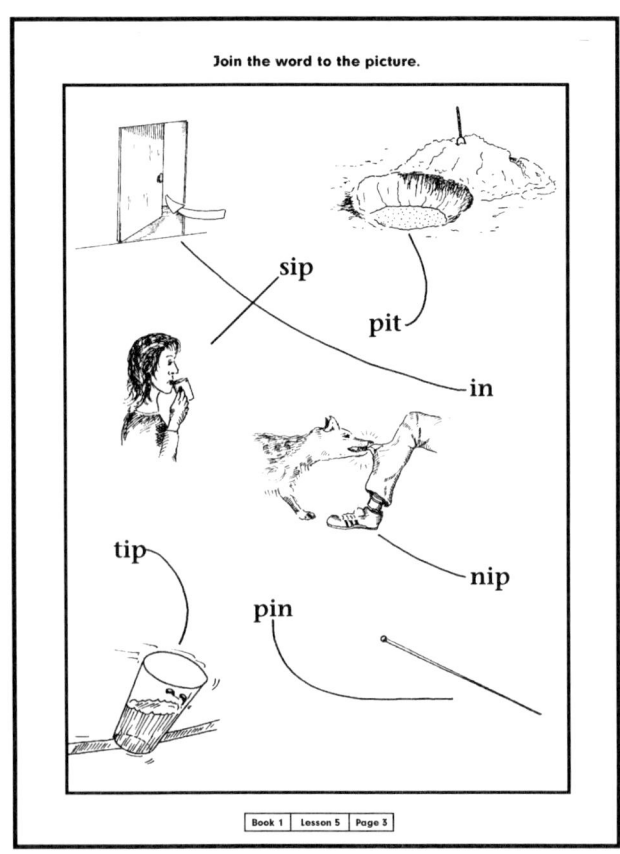
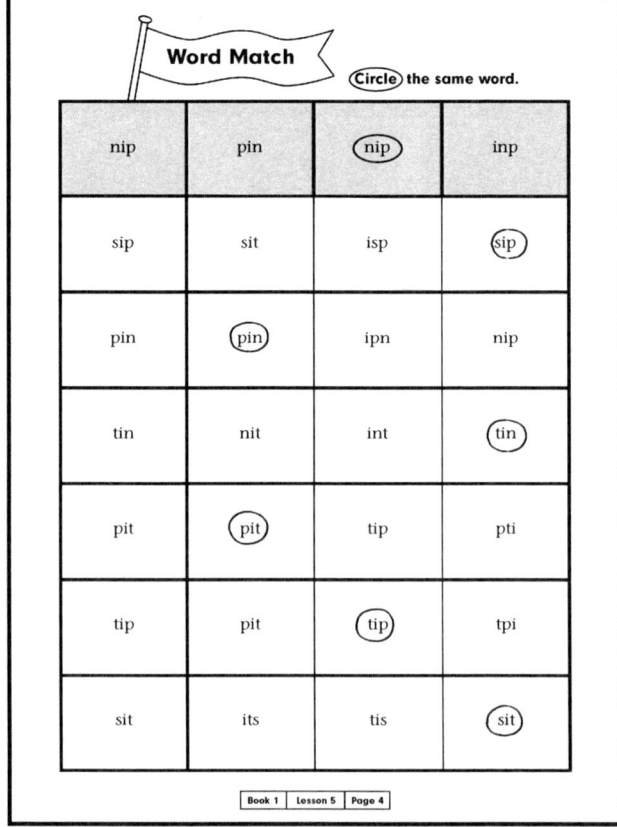

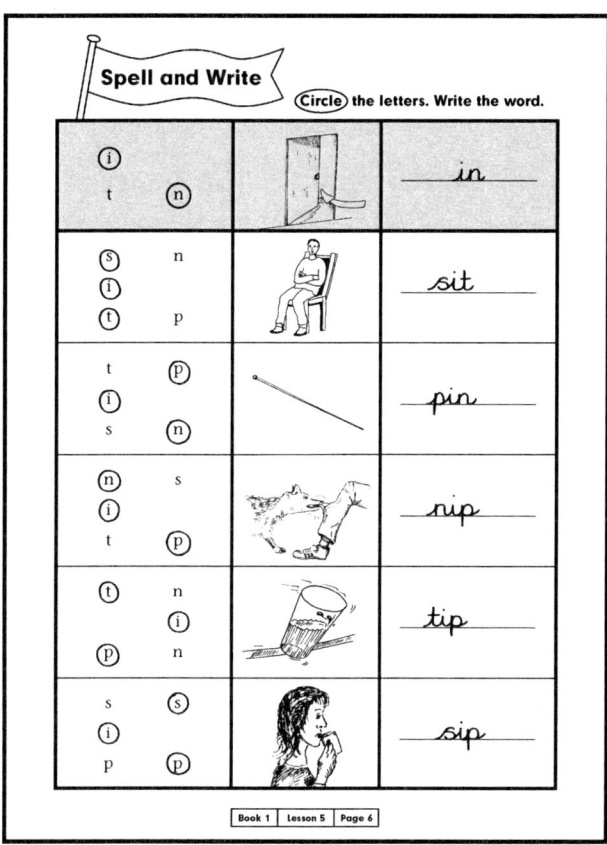
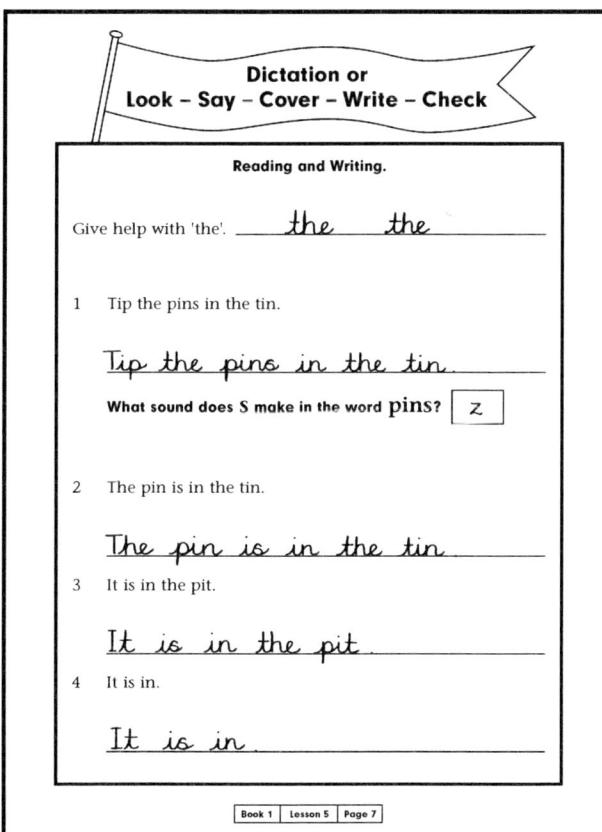
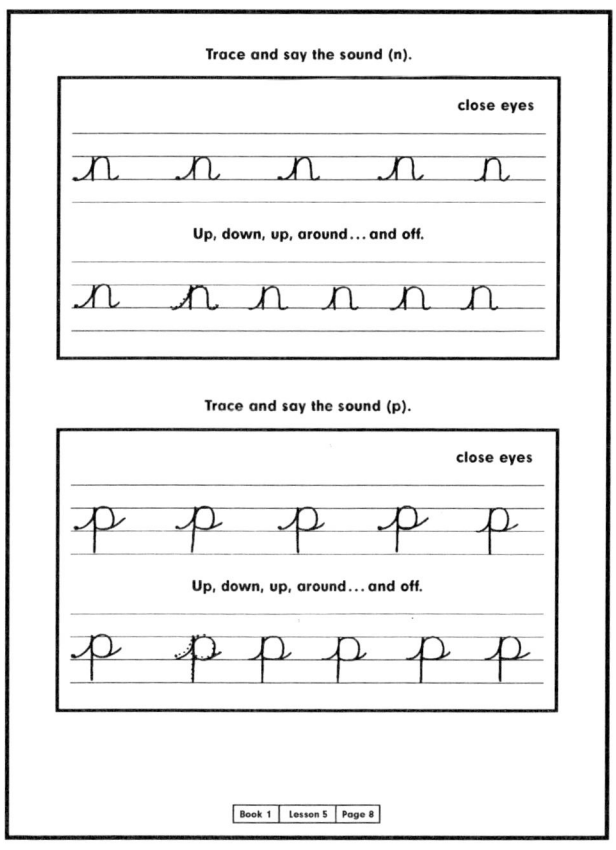

Answers to Lesson 6

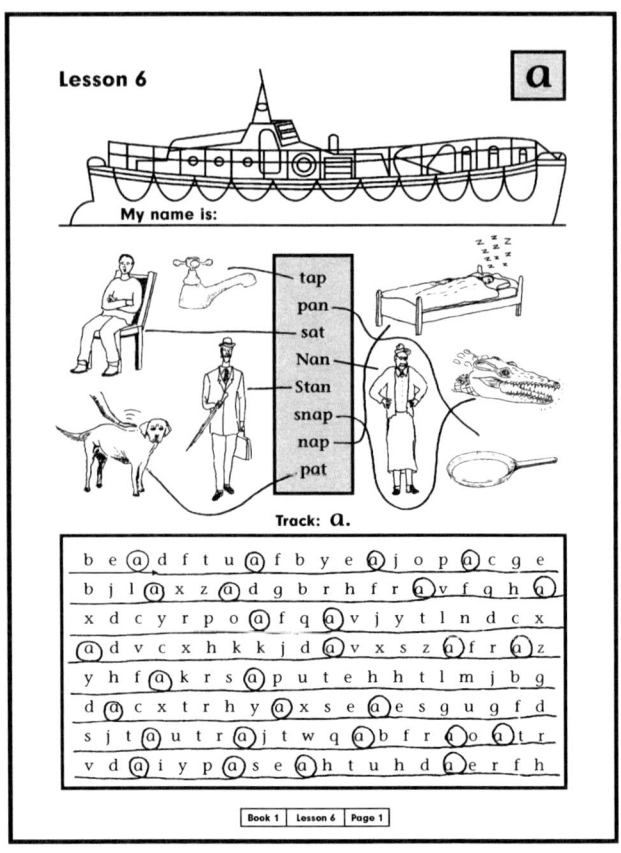

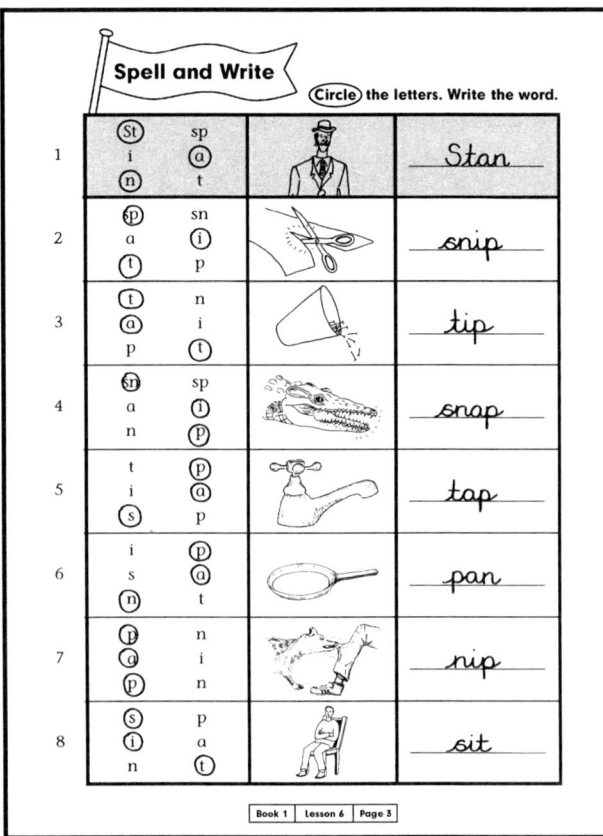

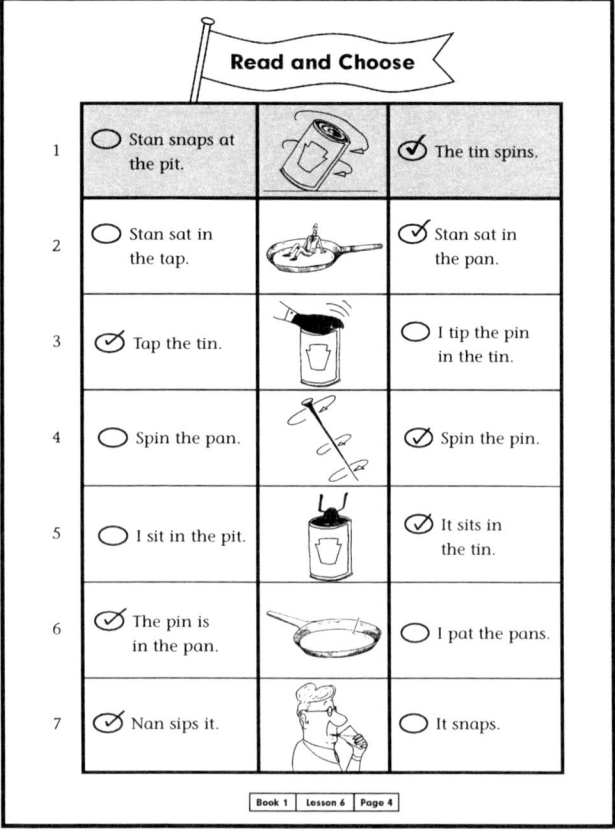

Dictation or Look – Say – Cover – Write – Check

1. Stan sat in the pan.
   Stan sat on the pan.
2. It spins in the tin.
   It spins in the tin.
3. I pat the pans.
   I pat the pans
4. Stan snips at it.
   Stan snips at it
5. Tip the pin in the tin.
   Tip the pin in the tin.

Handwriting – copy neatly.

a a a a
pat pat pat pat
asp asp asp asp
sat sat sat sat

Listening Skills

Circle the odd one out. Underline the same.

1	pan	(pat)	Nan
2	(spat)	snap	sap
3	sip	tip	(at)
4	(tin)	pit	sit
5	Stan	(tip)	tan
6	pins	spins	(naps)
7	spat	sat	(sap)
8	(snip)	tin	pin
9	tips	snips	(Stan)
10	taps	(sat)	naps

Cloze Procedure

1. Stan sat in the _pan_.
2. Is _Nan_ in the pit?
3. The _pin_ spins.
4. Nan _snips_ the tip.
5. Stan _taps_ Nan.
6. I _tip_ the pins in the pan.

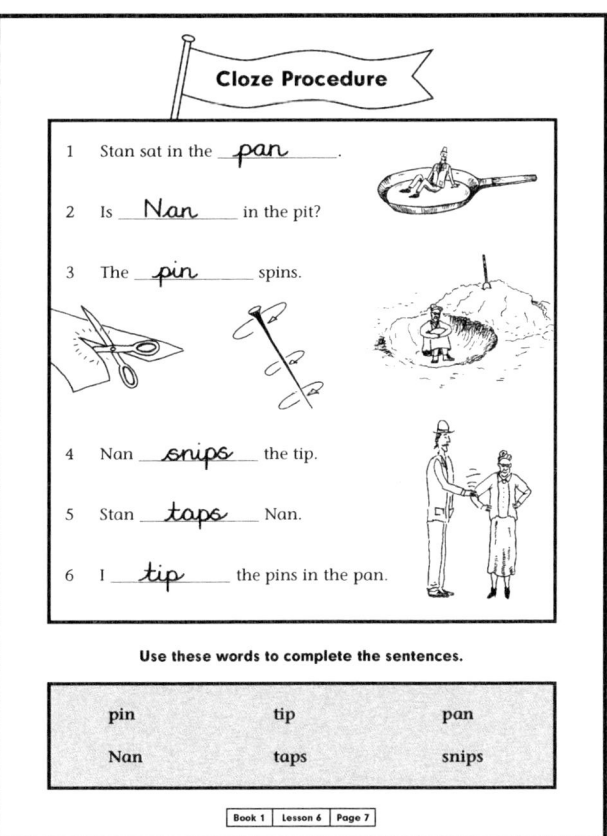

Use these words to complete the sentences.

pin	tip	pan
Nan	taps	snips

Wordsearch

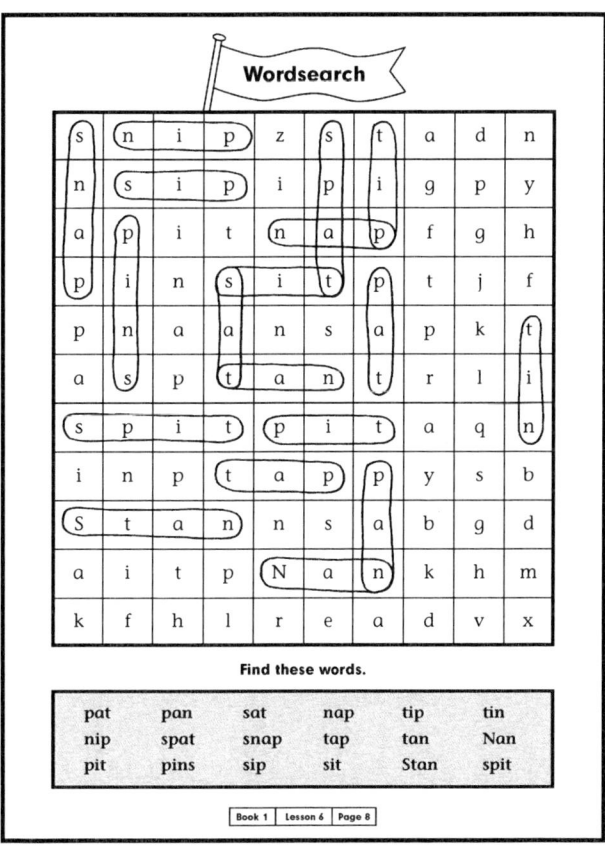

Find these words.

pat	pan	sat	nap	tip	tin
nip	spat	snap	tap	tan	Nan
pit	pins	sip	sit	Stan	spit

113

Answers to Lesson 7

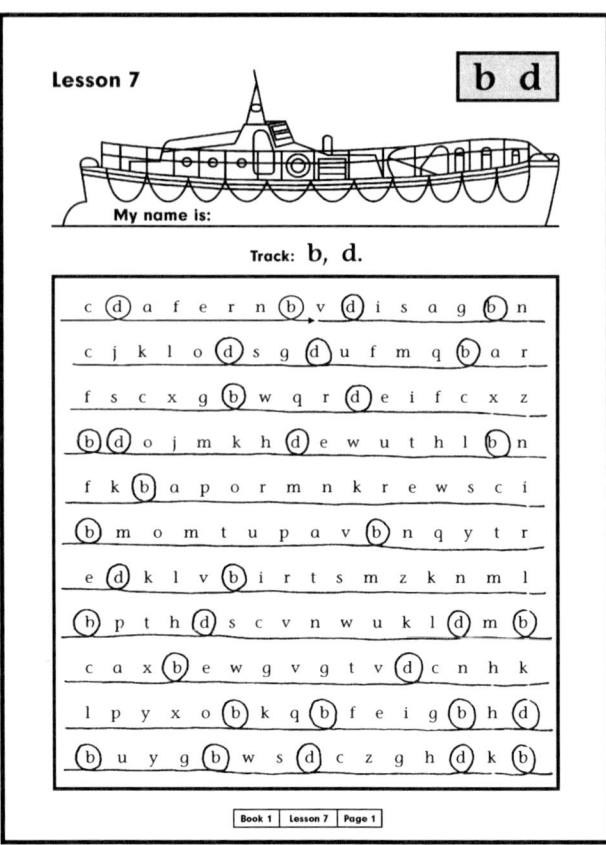
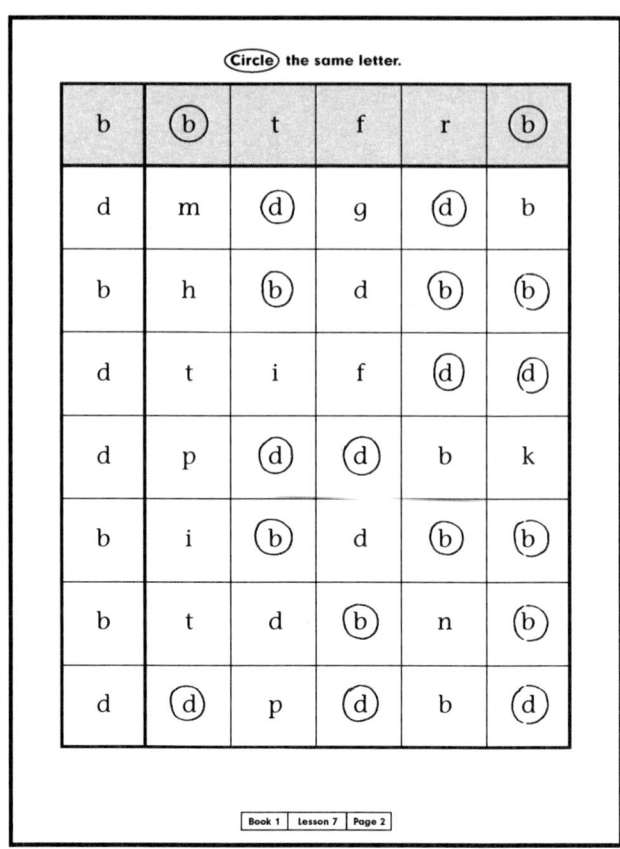
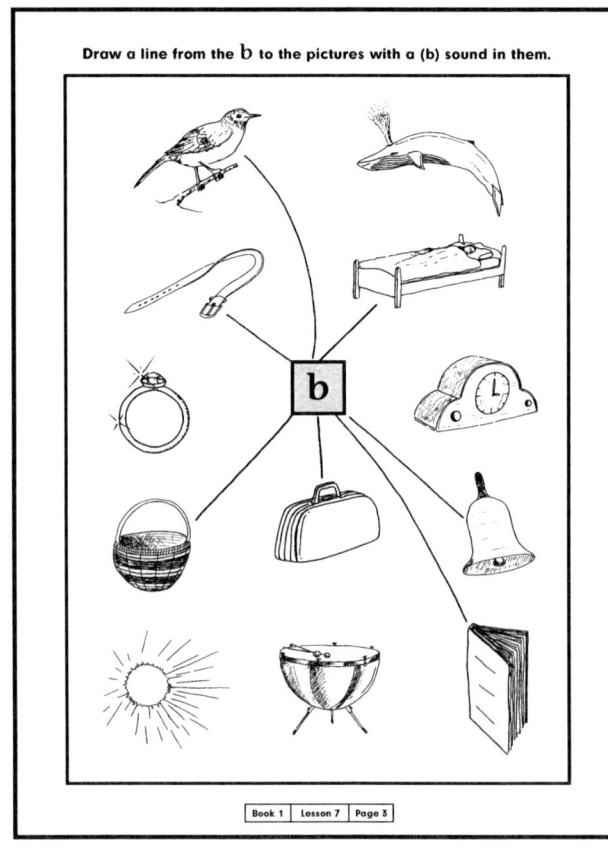
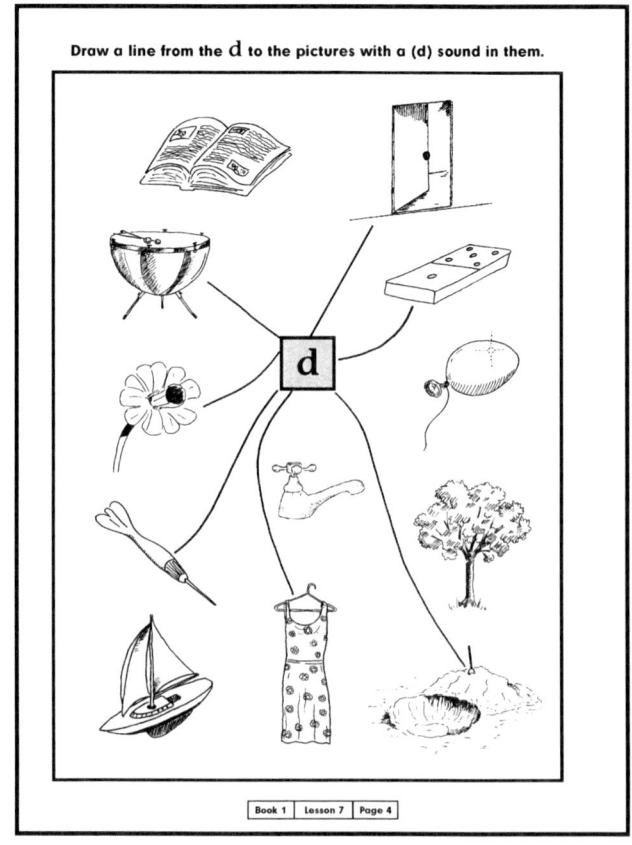

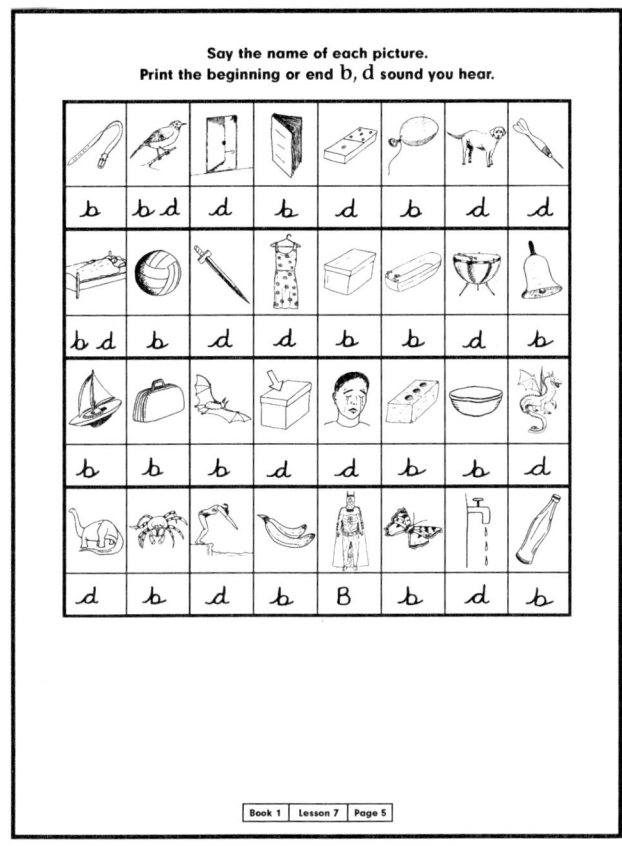

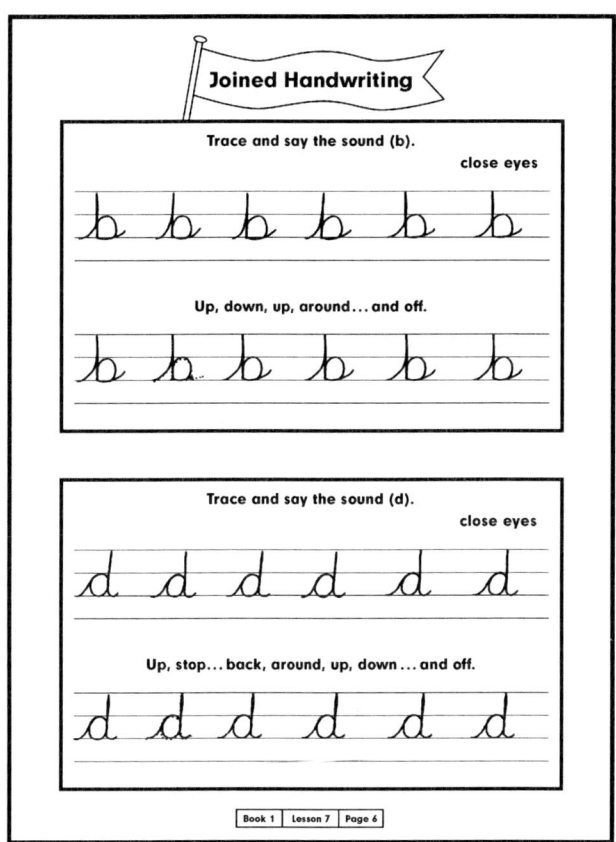

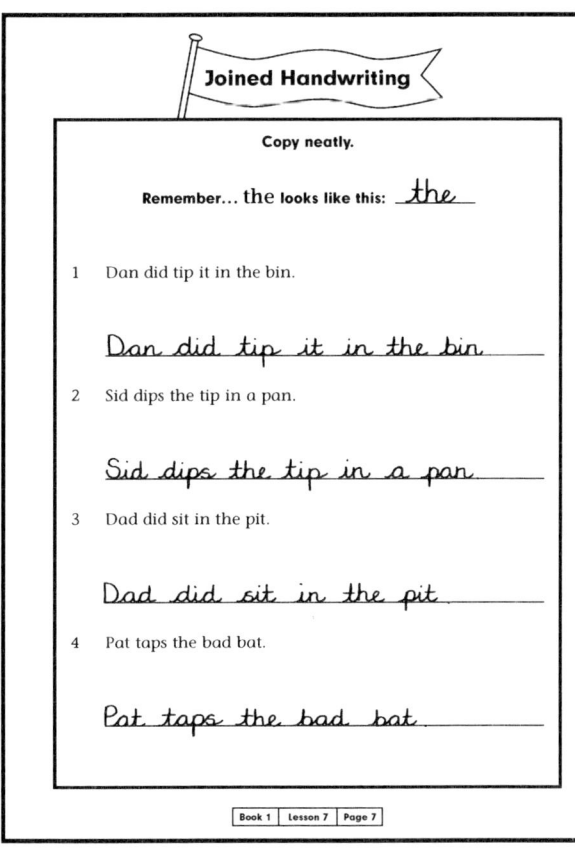

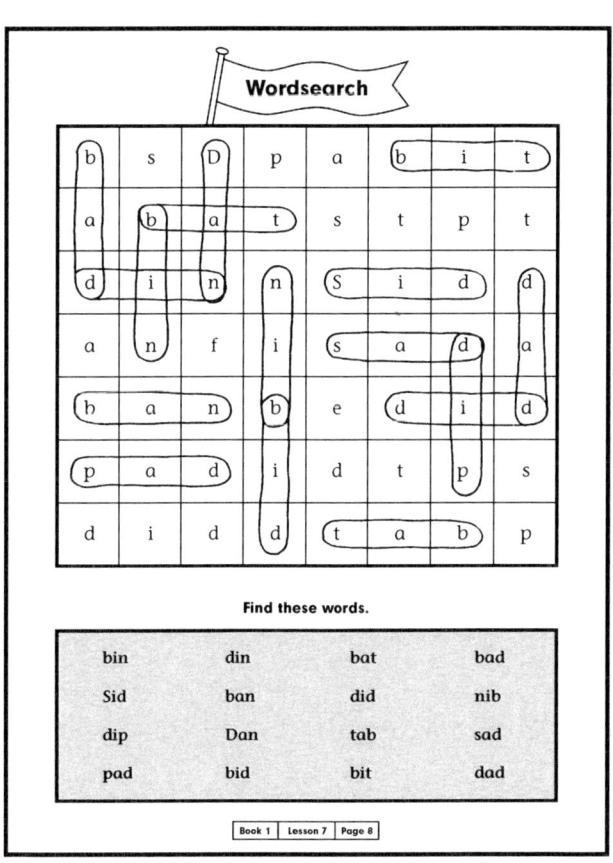

Answers to Lesson 8

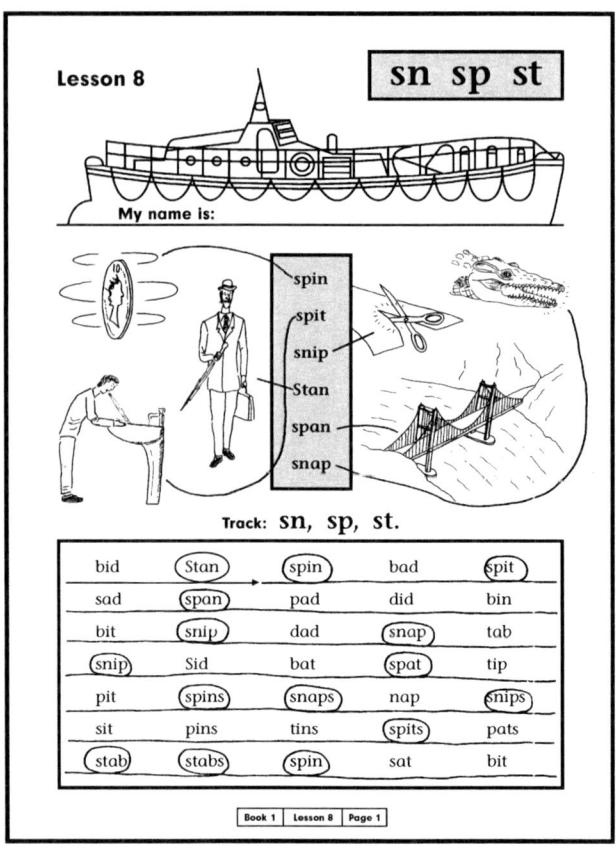
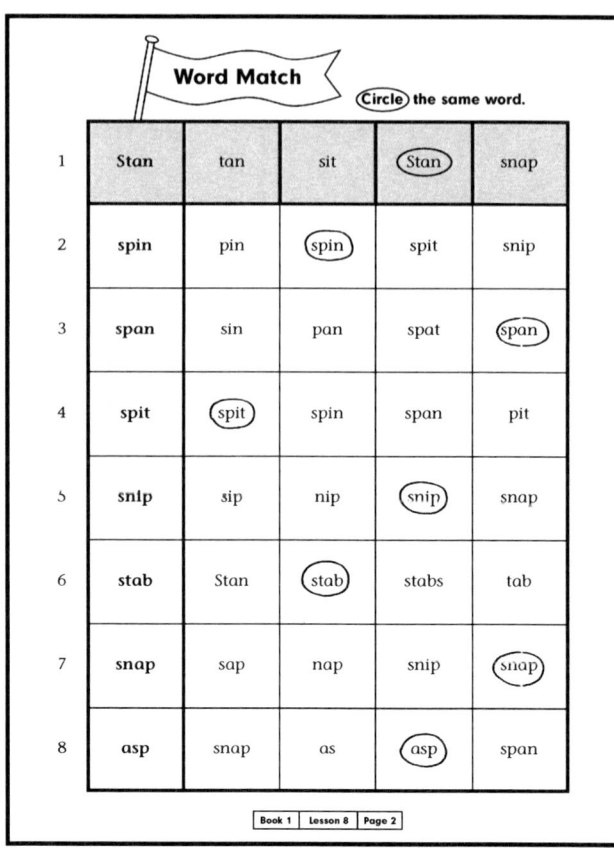
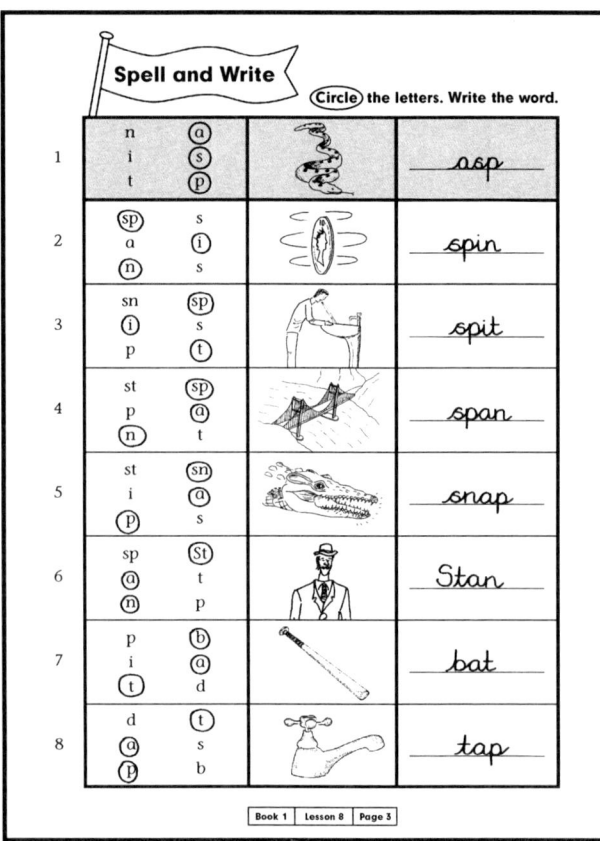
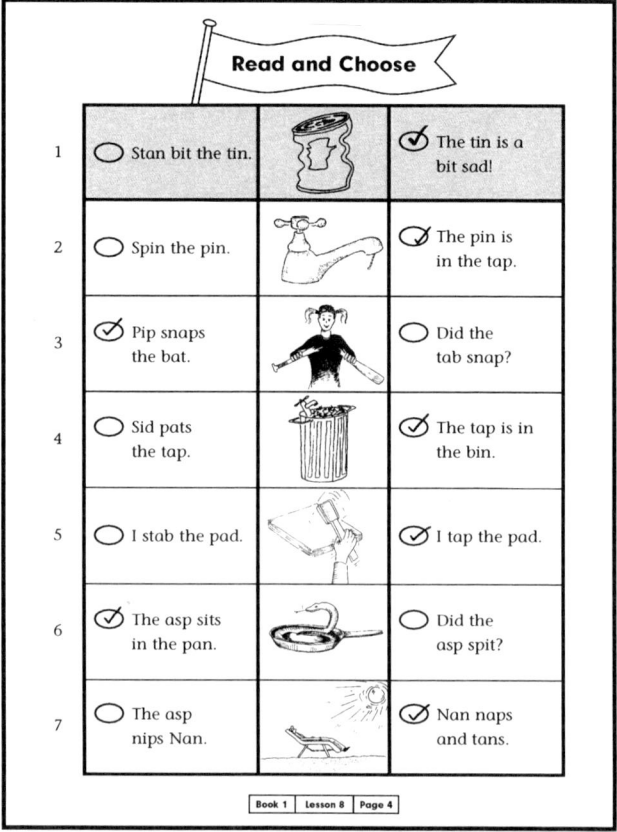

Dictation or Look – Say – Cover – Write – Check

1 Stan snips his pad.
Stan snips his pad.

2 Is a tap in the pit?
Is a tap in the pit?

3 Tip the pin in the tin.
Tip the pin in the tin.

4 Sid spits at the sap.
Sid spits at the sap.

Handwriting – copy neatly.

sp sp sp sp sp sp
st st st st st st
sn sn sn sn sn sn
asp asp asp asp

Listening Skills

Circle the odd one out. Underline the same.

1	snap	(tip)	nap
2	tip	snip	(nap)
3	(pad)	span	tan
4	spit	(bid)	sit
5	tab	stab	(span)
6	bid	Sid	(pan)
7	(stab)	dad	bad
8	bin	(span)	tin
9	tap	(snip)	sap
10	pan	Stan	(snap)

Cloze Procedure

1 *Stan* bit the tin.
2 *Spin* the pin.
3 Pat the *asp* spits *at* the tap.
4 Sad dad *tips* the *bin*.
5 Nan sits *in* the pit.
6 I *snap* the bat.

Use these words to complete the sentences.

asp	snap	Stan	tips
in	Spin	at	bin

Wordsearch

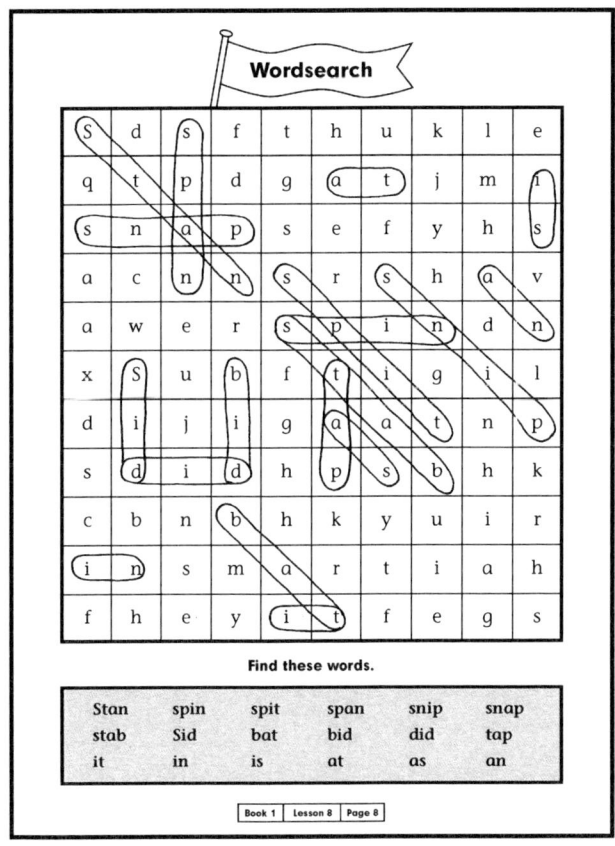

Find these words.

Stan	spin	spit	span	snip	snap
stab	Sid	bat	bid	did	tap
it	in	is	at	as	an

117

Answers to Lesson 9

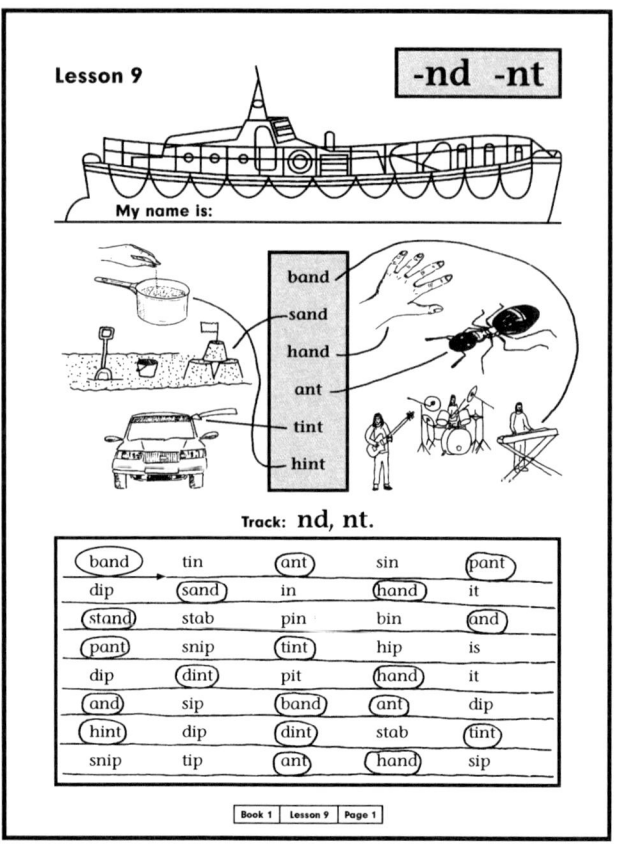
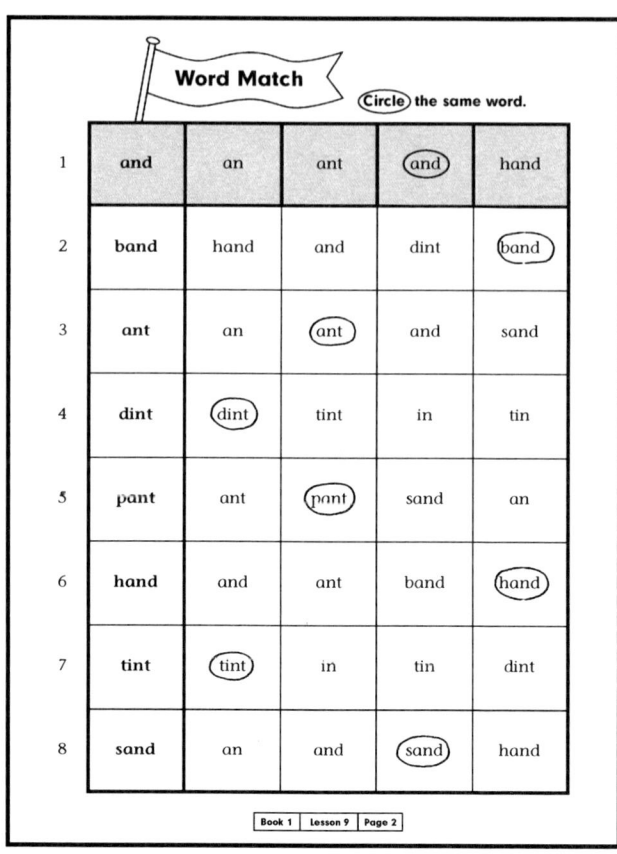
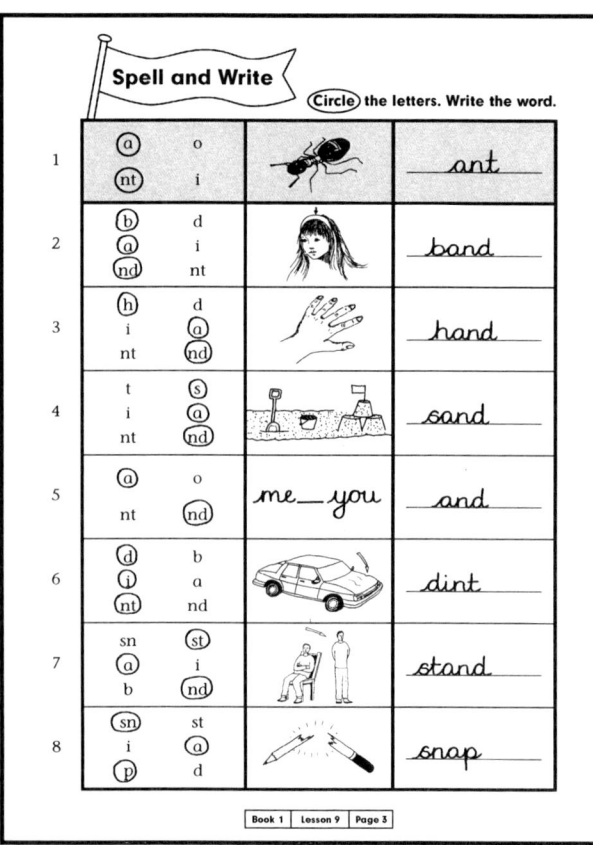
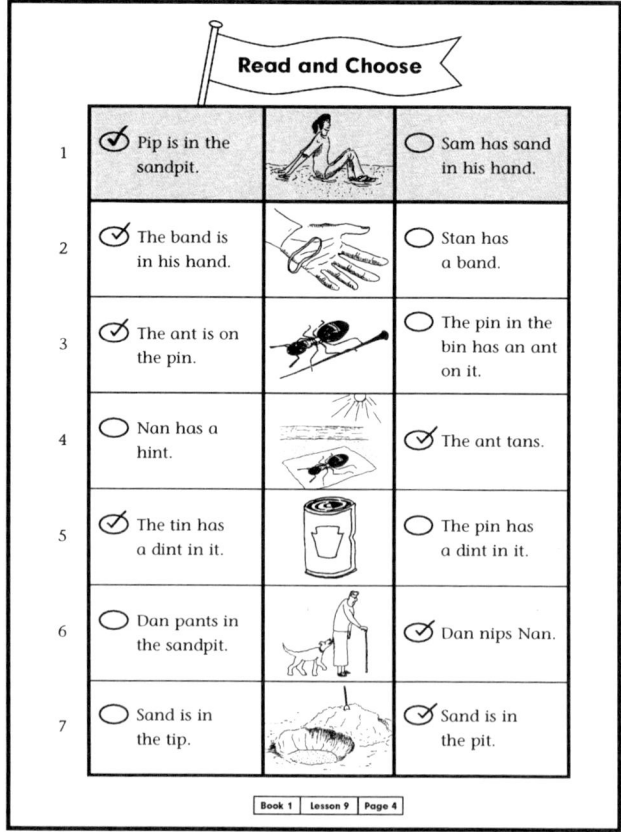

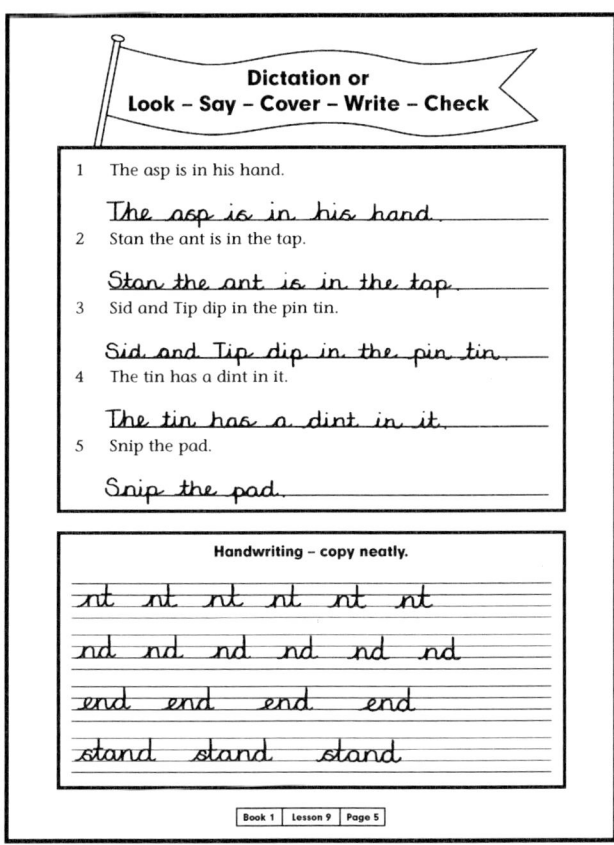

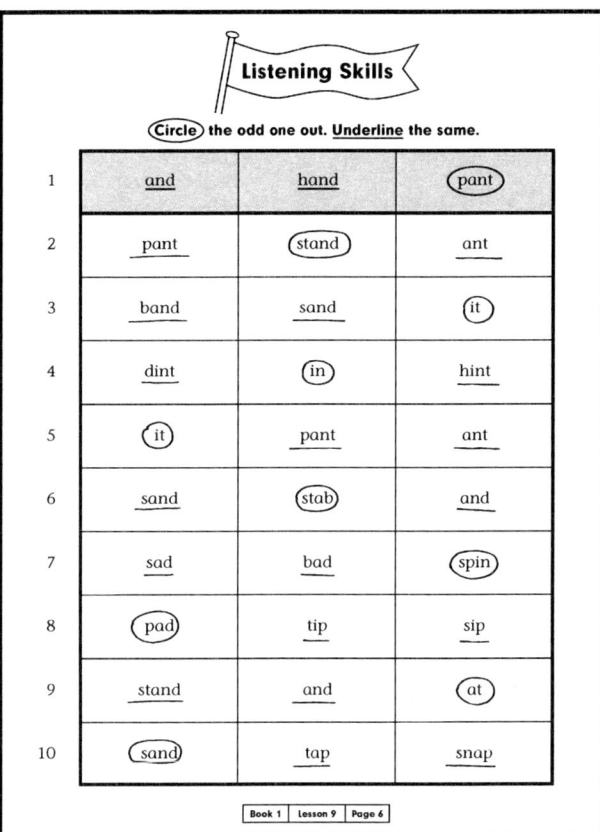

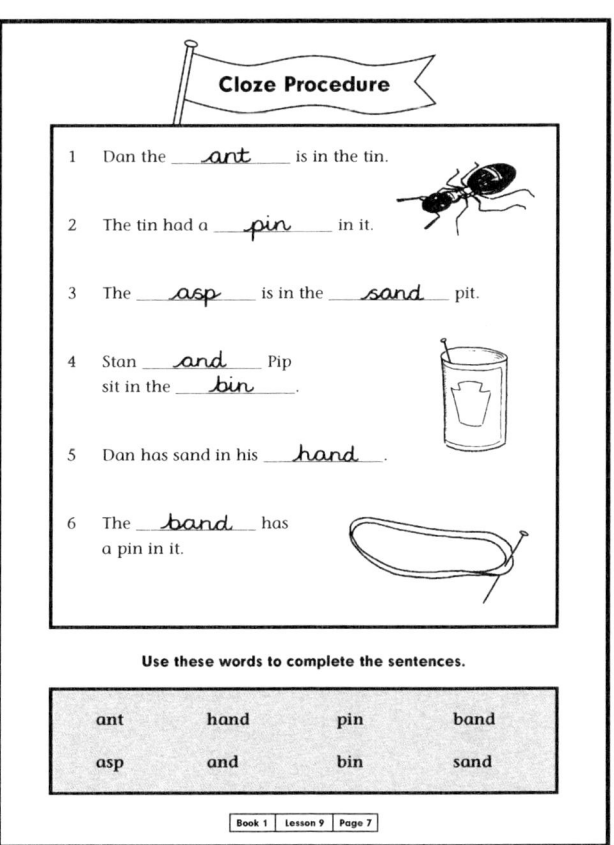

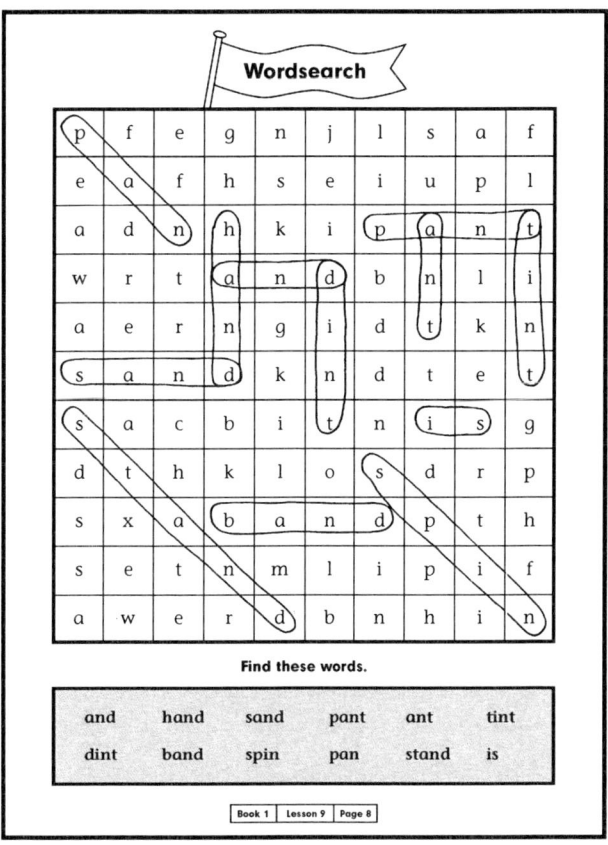

Answers to Lesson 10

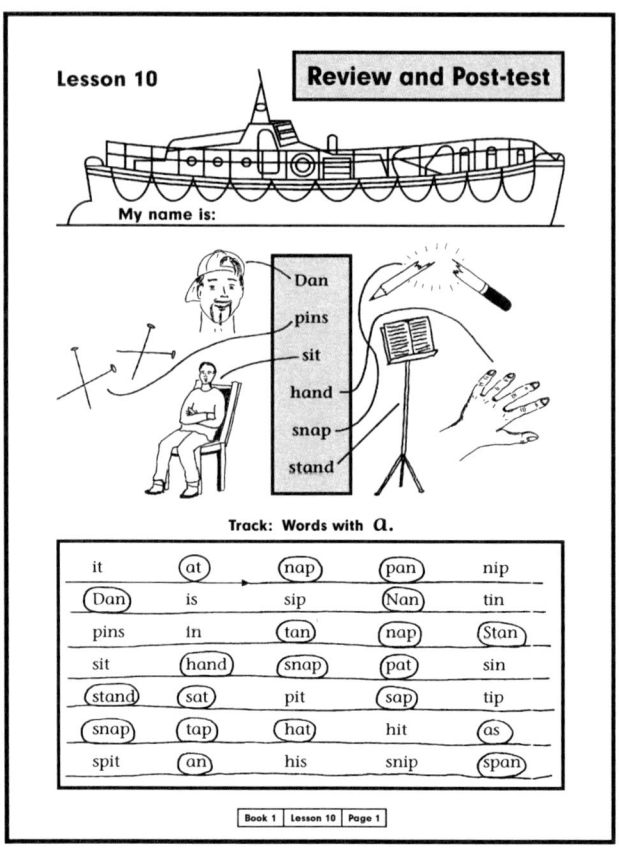
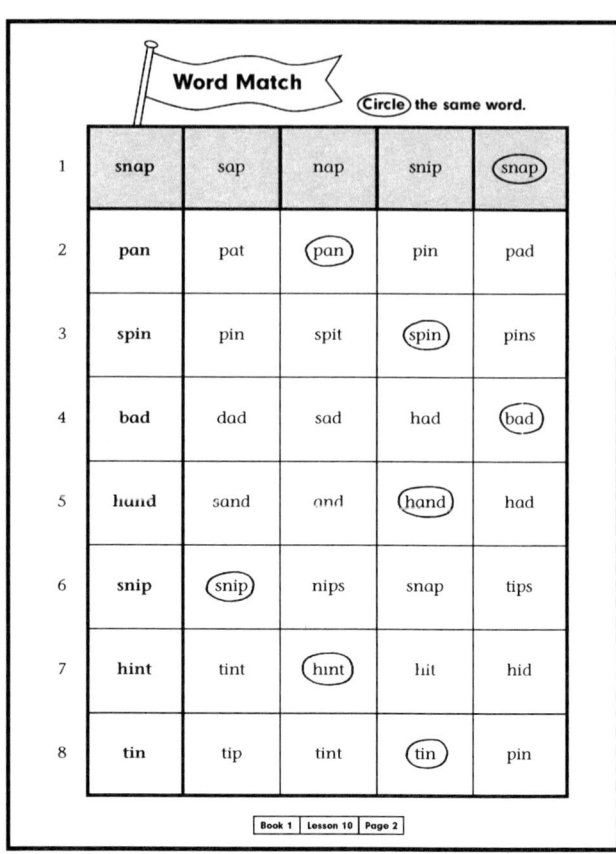
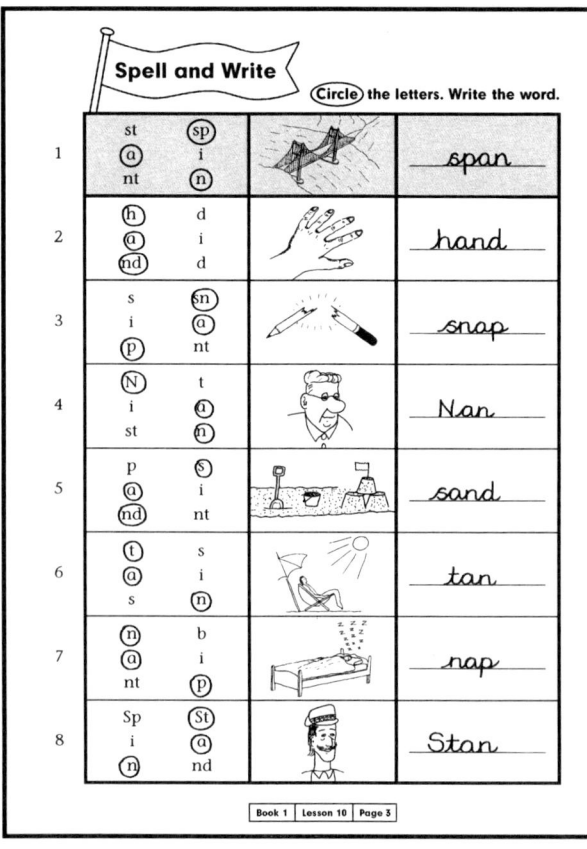
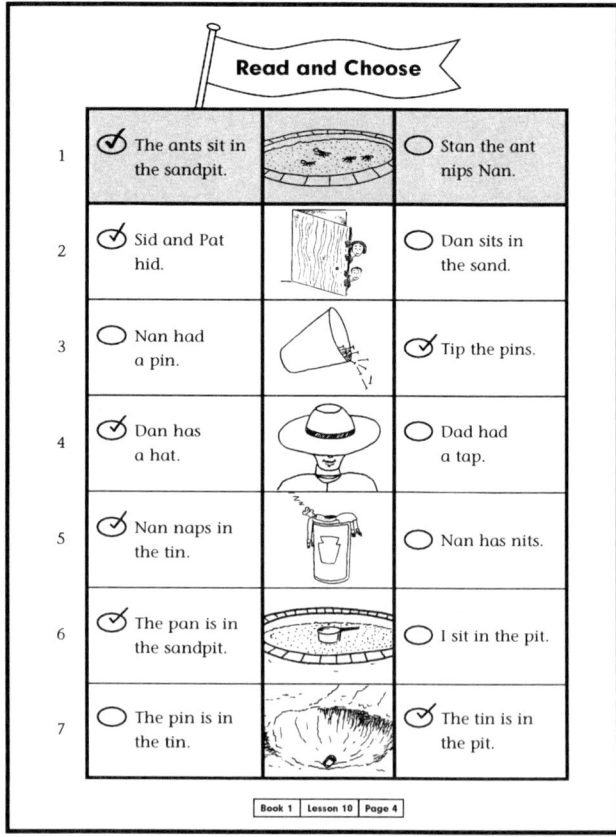

Dictation or Look – Say – Cover – Write – Check

1. Dan has ants in his pants.
   Dan has ants in his pants.
2. The asp sits in the sandpit.
   The asp sits in the sandpit.
3. Stan the ant hid in the tin.
   Stan the ant hid in the tin.
4. Dad has a band in his hat.
   Dad has a band in his hat.
5. Did Stan the ant nip Nan?
   Did Stan the ant nip Nan?

Handwriting – copy neatly.

i i i i i i i
st st st st st
a a a a a a
nd nd nd nd

Listening Skills

Circle the odd one out. Underline the same.

1	pin	pit	(pat)
2	sat	pat	(sit)
3	(Pip)	Nan	Stan
4	pant	ant	(and)
5	it	(an)	is
6	(ban)	did	Sid
7	as	at	(in)
8	sit	pit	(hid)
9	(tint)	hand	sand
10	nap	(spit)	tap

Cloze Procedure

1. Dan tips the _sand_.
2. Is _Nan_ in the pit?
3. Stan had a _tap_.
4. _Spin_ the pin in the _pan_.
5. Pip _dips_ his _hand_ in the pan.
6. Pat _hid_ the band in the tap.

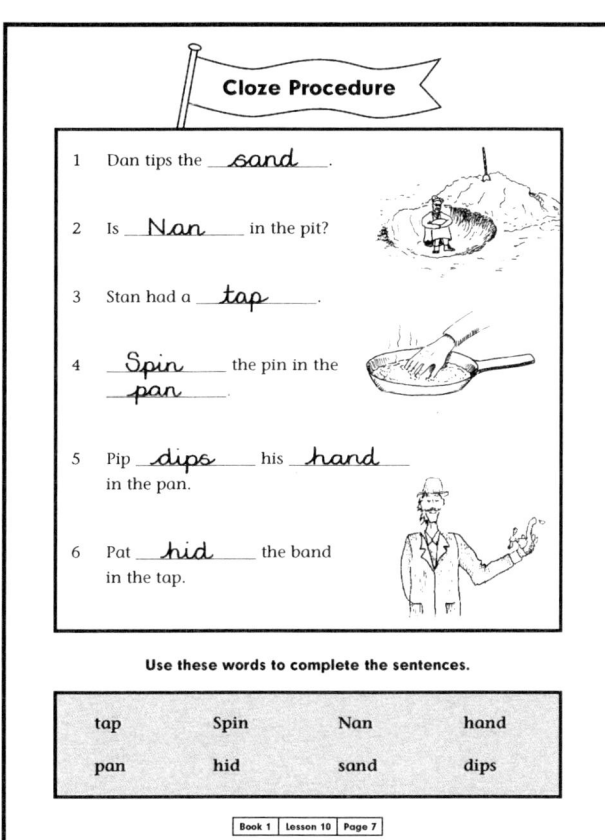

Use these words to complete the sentences.

tap	Spin	Nan	hand
pan	hid	sand	dips

Dot to Dot

Join the dots in the order of the alphabet: a b c d ...

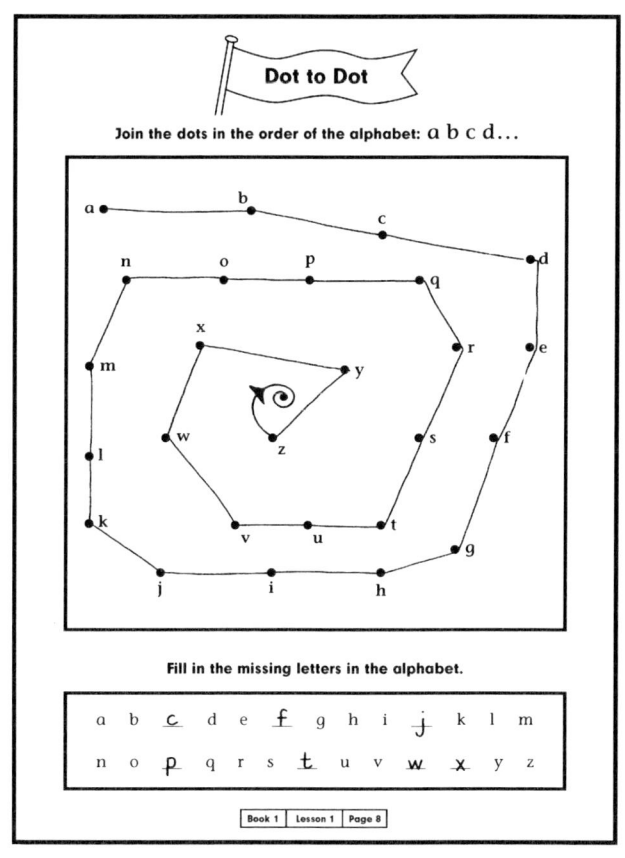

Fill in the missing letters in the alphabet.

a	b	c	d	e	f	g	h	i	j	k	l	m
n	o	p	q	r	s	t	u	v	w	x	y	z